LONDON'S SCOTTISH RAILWAYS
LMS & LNER

LONDON'S SCOTTISH RAILWAYS
LMS & LNER

A.J. MULLAY

TEMPUS

Frontispiece: Gresley's Pacifics operated in Scotland for over forty years, serving both the LNER and BR. Here, A3 No.2752 *Spion Kop* is seen receiving attention at King's Cross depot in June 1937, some thirteen years before she was transferred to Edinburgh's Haymarket. The last time the author saw this engine, she was in a woebegone state at neighbouring St Margaret's. (J & C McCutcheon)

First published 2005

Tempus Publishing Limited
The Mill, Brimscombe Port,
Stroud, Gloucestershire, GL5 2QG
www.tempus-publishing.com

British Library Cataloguing in Publication Data.
A catalogue record for this book is available from the British Library.

ISBN 0 7524 3480 2

Typesetting and origination by Tempus Publishing Limited
Printed in Great Britain

CONTENTS

Introduction

'The grouping of the railways should make the nation richer... it has made it so much easier and cheaper to transfer material or fuel or goods or persons from one part of the country to another'.

Arthur Mee's *Children's Encyclopedia*

If the Edwardian decade of 1901 to 1910 is looked on by historians as the Golden Age of Railways – when both passenger and shareholder could enjoy the benefits of a railway system operating at the peak of efficiency – the gold proved to be illusory. Within ten years, exhausted by a war of desperate attrition, Britain's railways were only too eager to grasp the idea of unification, or at least a reorganisation which would allow a pooling of resources, a centralisation of control – anything, in fact, which would preserve profits while maintaining some element of inter-company competition.

By 1918, the State had invaded the world of the private citizen. The British people were perfectly prepared to see their young men called up for compulsory military service, civil liberties suspended, and even the clocks being changed by order twice a year. Both the travelling public and the railways' employees – who constituted one of the biggest labour forces in the UK – had become accustomed to the idea of state control of Britain's railways. Railways came under the direction of the Railway Executive virtually as soon as war was declared in 1914, and continued – officially at least – until August 1921.

If nothing else, this should have confirmed the vital importance of Britain's railways, promoting a sense of gratitude in the bosom of the public, and of pride among railwaymen, for the rail system's undoubted contribution to victory. In fact, as discussed later in this book, exactly the opposite was to happen.

By the end of the First World War, there was a consensus among railway staff, stockholders and the public at large, that Britain's railways would have to undergo a substantial change in the way that they were constituted. Some amalgamations went ahead in the first four years after the war; the LNWR absorbed the Lancashire & Yorkshire, and the North Eastern the Hull & Barnsley, although both of these smaller companies were to be included in government legislation as independent entities.

Of the seventy or so major railway companies to be 'grouped', five were Scottish. There were, in order of size, the North British, Caledonian, Glasgow & South Western, Highland and Great North of Scotland. Their histories have all been written to varying extents, and the reader is referred to the Bibliography at the end of this book for more information. But the story of the 'big two' (London Midland & Scottish and London & North Eastern railways) has not been told in a Scottish context, and this book attempts to repair this omission.

The political history of the 1923 Grouping of Britain's railways centres on the meteoric rise of a certain Sir Eric Geddes. Described as Prime Minister Lloyd George's 'favourite technocrat', Geddes was born in India but raised in Edinburgh, and later boasted that he had been expelled from five public schools. He was employed in the United States as a railroad worker and occasional barman, before returning to the UK with even less money that he had left with. After more senior rail management experience in India, Geddes joined the North Eastern Railway, before being called into war service in 1914. So efficient was he, that he moved upwards from an administrative post in the army, taking over transport arrangements behind the front lines before being appointed as transport supremo for all war theatres. In this office he overcame the initial opposition of Field Marshal Haig to his appointment, so much so that the latter insisted on Geddes being given the rank of Major General.

As if this was not enough, Lloyd George asked Geddes to apply his much-admired business skills to improve the administration of the Admiralty. Within six months, Geddes was appointed First Lord, normally a political post, so he was made a Vice Admiral and was found a safe parliamentary seat. The position of First Lord of the Admiralty had been held by Churchill earlier in the First World War, and at the beginning of the Second World War. With his twin titles of Major General and Vice Admiral, Geddes could boast an 'unprecedented double' as John Grigg, Lloyd George's biographer, puts it. (Indeed, only Earl Mountbatten, in the Second World War, could claim a greater accumulation of working commissions.).

With the war won, Lloyd George was reinstalled following the 'khaki election' of December 1918, and promptly appointed Geddes Minister of Transport. This high-level appointment meant only one thing: that Geddes – with the backing of an admiring Prime Minister and, if nothing else, the grudging respect of his contemporaries – would be unstoppable in ensuring that times were to change on Britain's railways.

Despite his almost volcanic rise to the top, Geddes was a complex character, with at least two totally opposing characteristics. He showed no particular sympathy for working people, and was credited with preparing national anti-strike measures which the country, and particularly the railways, would see working at close hand in 1926. But he argued strongly – and ultimately in vain – for workers' representation in the company boardroom, a measure which the railway companies successfully cut out of the new transport legislation when Geddes was engaged on other work. (Curiously, it appears that the rail unions *also* opposed this plan, presumably as they assumed it was no more than a token gesture.). Had his plan been allowed to go ahead, the entire history of British industrial relations might have been different (and more harmonious) and the 1926 General Strike, whose extent shocked the managements of the LMS and LNER, less acerbic.

The resulting 1919 White Paper on railways proposed the establishment of seven groups, arranged geographically. They would comprise East, North East (effectively the NER as it already was), North West, South, West of England and Wales, Scotland and London local lines. The proposed survival of the NER virtually intact created opposition among those company chairmen and directors facing the loss of their influence in their own areas, although interestingly, it seems that Geddes could expect little thanks for his efforts on behalf of his old company. The historian Geoffrey Hughes records that Geddes appeared to have lost the confidence of the NER board following an enormous 'golden handshake' of £50,000, which he had received from the company to end its contractual relationship with him.

As far as our story is concerned, it should be noted that Geddes wanted to see the Scottish companies stay together in a group of their own, an idea dismissed by the companies themselves in the belief, unlikely to appeal to Scottish nationalists, that they would be unable to survive alone, unless they imposed higher rates per mile than in England.

Incidentally, there seems to have been little nationalistic opposition to the loss of control by Scots of their own railway companies. Many

shareholders in Scottish railways were non-Scots anyway, and the Edinburgh
& Glasgow and Caledonian Railways could not have been built, had they
not been seen as investment opportunities for English capital in the 1840s.
In 1923, the Scottish Home Rule Association prepared an open letter to the
Ministry of Transport on this matter (and rather late in the day), but their
claim of an 'overwhelming demand of the Scottish People for direct control
of their own affairs' was unsubstantiated, as the SHRA, not being a political
party, was not involved in the electoral process anyway. At least the association wanted to see 'friendly co-operation with English railway systems' if an
exclusively Scottish rail network had been attainable.

Some twenty-two years after Grouping, the Scottish National Party published a pamphlet called 'How Scotland lost its railways', with its author,
eccentric geologist Archie Lamont, arguing that the failure to set up an
exclusively Scottish railway in 1923 had caused duplication of services in
general, and of station facilities in particular. This was undeniable (although
not peculiar to Scotland), but Lamont rather spoiled his argument by
branching off into speculation about how the 1921 Act could have been
used as a springboard to build railways in remote areas, such as Durness in
Sutherland and Ullapool in Wester Ross. Such developments were surely
never likely in an age of burgeoning bus services.

That there was no major public reaction to the Grouping, north or south
of the border, should not be wondered at – public opinion had much less
influence on politicians than nowadays. There was no such thing as public
opinion polls; decisions affecting people's lives were taken just as often in
the boardroom as in the Commons chamber. Indeed, the United Kingdom
was not even fully democratic in 1923, some five years before female eman-
cipation was completed.

When Nationalisation followed in the late 1940s, the establishment of
a Scottish railway region within the British Railways system was a sign of
changing times in the history of British governance. The raft of legislation
brought in by the new Labour administration – nationalising coal, public
health, steel and railways – meant that both legislators and administrators
had to be fully aware of differences between English and Scottish legal systems and had to draft accordingly. But Scotland was below the horizon as
seen from Westminster in 1923, and the views of the Scottish Home Rule
Association – if they reached London at all – were not seen as significant.

When the Railways Bill eventually came before Parliament, the Eastern
and North Eastern groups were merged and the London lines omitted as
a separate unit, but the Scottish system was now to be divided into East

and West groups, both independent of the south. This proposal did not last long – it clearly did not answer concerns about possible higher conveyance rates – and the two Scottish groups were now simply added on to the two East and West Coast groups already proposed. What became the LMS and LNER were provisionally called the 'North West, Midland and West Coast Scottish' and the 'North East, East and East Scottish' groupings respectively. This is how the system looked when the Bill became an Act. At least it ensured that the East and West Coast main lines were now each run by a single company.

With two new companies now created as rival concerns connecting London with Edinburgh, Glasgow, Perth and Aberdeen over two main lines each more than 520 miles in length, the politicians left the railway community to fill in the fine detail on the new legal documents. This was because the political map had changed. Geddes had been transferred from the transport ministry to the new post of Chairman of the Committee on National Expenditure late in 1921, before leaving politics altogether in the following year, when Lloyd George lost his premiership. Railway personalities were perfectly happy to fill the vacuum left behind, and to take over the wheeling and dealing behind the scenes during this vital eighteen-month transitional period – none more so than Sir Guy Granet, the chairman of the Midland Railway, the largest single company making up the new LMS.

As we shall see, Granet was quick to secure an agreement with the Glasgow & South Western Railway, his company's working ally since 1876, doing so by effectively promising terms that would never be bettered. If such a promise was also made to the Highland, it is not immediately discernable in the company records, but that company was exhausted by the demands of the First World War, and unlikely to offer any major obstacle to amalgamation. Effectively, Granet isolated the Caledonian – an ally of the LNWR since the 1840s – and the allocation of only two directorships to the 'Caley' was a poor deal considering that the NBR obtained four seats in the LNER boardroom, including the most important seat of all.

The new company name 'London Midland & Scottish', summed up the geographical span of the new company. It included elements of the two largest companies, LNWR and Midland, in the title, and does not seem to have been a matter of contention. Over on the east, the choice of name was a greater subject of debate, with 'Great North Railway' a serious contender at one time (and reportedly the chairman's choice). Finally, the 'London and North Eastern Railway' was chosen, in December 1922, and soon compressed by the loss of the 'and'. In any event, the company's critics were later to daub it the 'Late and Never Early'!

Dr Hughes, in his company history of the LNER, suggests that the 'North Eastern' part of the title refers to the whole of Great Britain – to compensate for the lack of any Scottish element in the title – but that seems unlikely, more probably being simply a nominal tribute to the largest company in the new group (just as the name 'Midland' featured over on the LMS). When administrative divisions were subsequently named on the LNER, the 'North Eastern Area' certainly did not pertain to Aberdeenshire! It was a curious title for an administrative unit which was roughly halfway down the map of the entire system, and its title can only be seen as a concession to those of the former NER persuasion.

1

Farewell under a Full Moon

For Patrick Ransome-Wallis, the New Year's Eve party of 31 December 1922 was more than just the usual annual 'knees-up'. In his words, 'the most momentous happening was to take place at midnight… yet people went on dancing and drinking and eating as though this was just another New Year!'

This young railway enthusiast had good reason to feel personally aggrieved at the coming Amalgamation of Britain's railways; his parents had refused him the chance of an apprenticeship under Nigel Gresley at Doncaster works, as the great man could not offer any guarantees about the youngster's career prospects to Ransome-Wallis senior.

Whether his parents' caution was justified is a moot point. The Grouping of British railways into four major consortia from 1 January 1923 proved to be less than earth-shattering, with little outward appearance of any trans-formation, particularly at first. Overall, there was a feeling that things would have to change, but not by all that much. No railwaymen lost their jobs, and most company directors made a very great deal of money in the short-term.

The final entry in the minute-book of the North British Railway Board of Directors summarises the last of their meetings, held on 2 March 1923. It is a routine entry, simply listing approval of previous minutes and a report of business being prepared for the last Annual General Meeting, to be held later that day.

There was no ceremonial 'signing-off'. This most unglamorous of rail-way companies, the largest in Scotland, terminated its activities in the same no-nonsense businesslike way it ran its affairs during its eighty years of existence.

The NBR had been in a difficult position in relation to government control. As the largest Scottish rail concern, it had acted as the 'secretary' Scottish company to the government during the war, and inevitably became involved in a number of administrative problems and conflicts. Day-to-day liaison with the military authorities had been conducted by Maj. Stemp, formerly of the Royal Engineers. Charles Hubert Stemp had made a name for himself on the Great Eastern Railway and was headhunted by the NBR around the turn of the century. Once installed in Edinburgh, he was responsible for implementing the Control scheme (unique in Scotland) introduced with the opening of the new Lothian Lines, and which was an immediate success. One suspects that, had Stemp not been conducting the company's relations with the Military, these might have been a great deal worse! In particular, the Ministry was painfully slow in paying secretarial dues to the company, at a time when the latter badly needed new financial investment in permanent way and rolling stock. Geddes, on the other hand, let it be known that he found NBR accounting to be baroque in its complexity.

Some English transport historians have alleged that the NBR all but ceased to introduce new main-line locomotives after the war, leaving the 'Sassenachs' to deal with the problem of an ageing locomotive fleet. This ignores the fact that 'Scotts', 'Glens', passenger tank engines and two new Atlantics were being introduced as the 1920s dawned – a considerable outlay for a cash-strapped company. If the NBR did deserve criticism, it was perhaps in its less-than impressive signalling system, with no departmental status within the company.

Despite the conflicts generated by its 'secretarial' status, the NBR accepted the principle of the Grouping as it was called – the setting-up of four super-companies on 22 December 1922 – agreeing to give to its bankers 'authority to transfer all monies, deposits, bills of exchange, drafts, promissory notes, securities, and all other instruments of credit' to the new company, which soon was to assume the name of the London & North Eastern Railway. (One wonders if the board members would have been so compliant, if they could have foreseen the new company's refusal, unique among the 'Big Four', to declare any dividend for ten successive years from 1935!).

The North British was to enter this East-Coast group as the second-largest company (after the North Eastern, in mileage terms) along with the Great Northern, Great Eastern, Great Central, Hull & Barnsley and Great North of Scotland. Of twenty-six proposed members of the new LNER board of Directors, the NBR accepted an invitation to nominate four. The names forwarded were: William Whitelaw (NBR chairman since 1918), Messrs Gray, McCosh and Murray. All were to make their mark in the LNER. The new company was eventually to name a streamlined A4 Pacific after two (Whitelaw and Andrew K. McCosh), and less glamorous B1 4-6-0s after the other two (Murray of Elibank and Alexander Reith Gray). There was also a new Scottish Area Local Committee. (Its title tended to vary, and its importance was questionable, as will be discussed later.).

In particular, the appointment of William Whitelaw as chairman of the new company was a massive compliment, both to him personally, and to the North British. Whitelaw had chaired the Highland Railway until 1912, and his tenure at the NBR earned him a reputation as a fair-minded individual with a good grasp of detail and unapproachable integrity (qualities not always found in company directors!).

Whitelaw's reputation had been enhanced during the run-up to the Grouping, when the company was in conflict with the Ministry of Transport over a financial matter. The Minister, Sir Eric Geddes, is believed to have ordered the 'leaking' of correspondence between himself and the NBR chairman, something which simply did not usually happen in those days, and which showed up Geddes as something less than a gentleman. After that, Whitelaw was a popular choice for the LNER chair!

In this day and age of multinational conglomerates, it is easy to forget just how important Britain's four grouped railways were to the national economy and workforce, and as a consequence what a compliment Whitelaw's appointment was. In his book *LNER* – and a better, more readable, history of the company would be hard to find - Geoffrey Hughes compares the LMS and LNER with other British companies of the time. The LNER, with an issued capital of £348 million, was not far behind the LMS with £400 million (at 1923 prices – multiply by twenty-five for today's). No other British company at the time topped £50 million, and the largest steel concern was worth only £8 million. The chief executive of the Post Office earned £3,000 per annum, and the head of the civil service £500 more. In contrast, Sir Ralph Wedgwood, the new Chief General Manager of the LNER, was pulling down £10,000 a year! As if in recognition of the gravity of this appointment, Wedgwood was knighted almost as soon as he was in post.

This indicates the scale of Whitelaw's appointment. The valediction he received at the NBR's final AGM, on 2 March 1923, was extraordinary, with his deputy chairman, the Duke of Buccleuch, telling the assembled stockholders, 'he has been one whom we not only respect, but love'. History has remembered Whitelaw – and his grandson, of the same Christian name, a minister in recent Conservative governments who died as recently as 1999 – while Sir Eric Geddes is unheard of nowadays.

An interesting footnote about the two William Whitelaws concerns the younger of that ilk, the cabinet minister of the same name during the Thatcher years. Apparently, on one occasion the station management at Aberdeen assumed that the young Whitelaw who phoned to make travel arrangements was actually the chairman, and the young man was personally escorted to the train by the stationmaster. Once aboard he found a bottle of finest malt left in his compartment! The grandson failed to point out the mistake, but later received a 'roasting' from his grandfather, far greater than, in his words, 'anything Margaret Thatcher doled out'! Moreover, he was told not to let his grandmother find out about the whisky! Incidentally, a new biography (see Bibliography) omits any mention of Whitelaw's chairman-ship of the NBR, stating categorically that his role as Highland Railway chairman up to 1912 qualified him for his elevation to the LNER!

As with the North British Railway, there was no great fuss made at the final meeting of the directors of the Great North of Scotland, the only other major Scottish rail concern being absorbed into the LNER. Final acceptance of amalgamation conditions was agreed at a meeting of proprie-tors and stockholders on 17 November 1922, with the following 1 January described as the 'day of vestment'. Not a surprising term, perhaps, for the date of the handover, considering that the GNSR chairman, Alexander Duffus, was an advocate (the equivalent of an English barrister). Duffus was nominated to the new LNER board as the only representative of the former GNSR, although, unfortunately, he died within fifteen months.

With its 172 locomotives (no fewer than 150 of them tender engines), and its 526 track-miles, the Great North was a compact and hardworking system. It was deservedly proud of its hotel ownership – it operated the Palace and Station Hotels in Aberdeen, and the Cruden Bay establishment, complete with golf course and tramway connecting with the Boddam branch. The records show that all three hotels comfortably turned in a profit at the time of Grouping, but that the golf course was making a loss!

Trustingly, no less than £2,000 was placed into an Aberdeen bank account with Duffus and one other director as signatories, 'to meet possible contingencies in connection with staff changes and otherwise'. Curiously, the GNSR files for November 1922 also show that the company was able to lend no less than £23,000 to Fife County Council for a month at 3 per cent interest.

The company's inclusion in the new East-Coast group had more than a little to do with its traditional animosity with the Highland. It would have been logical for the GNSR to have entered the new LMS; after all, it had no physical connection with its new colleagues in the LNER, whose metals ended at Kinnaber Junction, 38 miles south of Aberdeen.

In contrast to all this, the Caledonian Railway resolved to fight the Grouping. It was alone in this defiance, certainly in Scotland. Its traditional rival, the Glasgow & South Western, had approved of the idea of amalgamation as early as 3 October 1922, the first Scottish company to do so. Chairman Lord Glenarthur and his fellow directors had managed to extract from the Midland and LNWR Railways the intriguing promise that those companies, 'will not offer any other constituent company better relative terms than those agreed with the GSW company'. No wonder the Caledonian, a much bigger concern, was so incensed! And the records indicate that the railway directors themselves, principally Sir Guy Granet of the Midland, were particularly active in smoothing the path towards amalgamation. (Granet went on to chair the new LMSR for four years from 1924.).

On a practical level, it is interesting to see that the Midland had been so impressed with the work of the G&SWR General Manager, David Cooper, that it specifically asked that he join the (supervisory) Scottish Committee being set up by the new company. This was formally agreed at the last meeting of the 'South West' board on 28 February 1923, when Cooper's contract of employment – signed only four years previously – was terminated with a lump payment to Cooper of no less than £7,500. The Minutes make it clear that this in no way compromised the payment of his pension of £2,356, to be paid annually to him. (Unfortunately, O.S. Nock believed that Cooper's retirement removed a strong, competent, personality who could have stood up to undesirable 'Caledonian' influences on the new LMS Northern division.). The enormous sums settled on Cooper were not only an index of his loss to the new company, but were a pleasant change to the usual bonanzas paid to company directors at this time. In the case of the G&SW directors, £10,000 was voted to them by the shareholders, because, 'they suffered loss by abolition of office'.

Lord Glenarthur had been a popular chairman, already enjoying the unusual distinction of having a locomotive named after him on a line which otherwise hardly went in for naming at all. At the last board meeting, Glenarthur was presented by his fellow directors with a silver George III cup. He replied by saying that, 'when he joined the board more

than 22 years ago, Sir James Bell told him that he would never find a pleas-
anter board on which to serve, and certainly his experiences justified that
prediction', as the Minutes record.

Although the Scottish companies were later accused by some English
railwaymen – and more recently by transport historians – of skimping on
maintenance and rolling stock replacement once the Grouping was finalised,
this was certainly not true of the old Glasgow & South Western Railway.
After purchasing 4,200 tons of steel rails from Colvilles for laying in the
year 1922, the order for the following year was actually increased to 6,000
tons at £8 7s 6d per ton, with a further 2,000 tons to be acquired, 'if these
can be bought on the same terms'.

So, in the words of the G&SWR unofficial historian, David L. Smith:
'1922 went out peacefully under a full moon. So also went the old Sou'
West'.

Like the G&SWR, the Highland Railway had accepted the Amalgamation
with resignation, if not enthusiasm. As already observed, the company had
been brought almost to the point of exhaustion by the heavy traffic of both
naval personnel and warship coal threading its way through the entire system, from Perth right up to the far north.

Other companies had loaned locomotives to the Highland from the start
of the conflict, while the company's attempts to introduce a new powerful class of 'River' 4-6-0s proved disastrous, with the Highland's own civil
engineer banning their introduction. The locomotives' designer, F.G. Smith,
was forced to resign. This was somewhat draconian, there being no loss
on the financial account, as the Highland shrewdly sold the engines on to
the Caledonian at a profit. Interestingly, by 1928, the LMS was to reintro-
duce the 'Rivers' back onto the metals they were designed to traverse, and
they did so without mishap. One aspect of railway management where the
Highland excelled was in their hotel chain, with successful establishments at
Achnasheen, Inverness, Strathpeffer, Kyle, and Dornoch.

Nevertheless, directors and staff must have been under no illusion that,
as part of a national transport artery, the old Highland Railway would
require new investment and capital. Not surprisingly, the stockholders
passed a unanimous motion on 24 November 1922, accepting the concept of Amalgamation. One Highland director, Mr A.E. Pullar (of Perth)
was nominated to the new LMS board, and two others, including company chairman W.H. Cox of Snaigow, to the Scottish Local Committee. The
curiously exact sum of £4,512 was to be disbursed among the directors for
the inconvenience of their loss of office.

When the 'wrapping-up' meeting of shareholders was held in Inverness on 28 February 1923, one speaker mentioned the appointment of the Highland's former chairman, William Whitelaw, to the similar position at the new LNER. The speaker was interrupted by applause, so popular did Whitelaw remain, years after leaving the company. It was an indicator of the 'family' atmosphere which characterised the old Highland Railway.

This was reflected in a Special Notice sent out by Traffic Manager Thomas McEwan to his staff at the beginning of the last week of the Highland Railway's existence. It is worth quoting from as it addressed the concerns about job security which must have confronted rail staff on the Highland, as elsewhere (and these could surely have been answered earlier than the last week of 1922. In fairness to senior management, their own future was also unknown at this time.).

On Monday next, 1st January, the Highland Railway will become part of the London, Midland and Scottish Railway… you will be officially advised as soon as the Management of the Highland Section has been definitely settled. In the meantime I am asked to carry on as at present, and you will therefore, until further notice, report to me as usual.

I appeal to all members of the Traffic Staff to demonstrate, by every means in their power, that in taking over the Highland Railway, the new Group have got possession of a live concern, serving a wide district which under progressive management, is capable of great development… With cordial greetings and best wishes for the new year.

Despite their positive acceptance of Amalgamation, and, surprisingly, in view of the assurances given to the G&SWR, the two smaller Scottish constituents of the new LMS were not particularly well represented in the boardroom. Each had only one director (Kerr from the 'South West', and Pullar from the Highland). Meanwhile, only two seats were being reserved for the Caledonian – compared to twelve for its ally, the LNWR, combined with the Lancashire & Yorkshire. A 1922 document entitled the 'Preliminary Amalgamation Scheme', and preserved in the National Archives, records that all directors must personally own £2,500-worth of shares in the new company, and that the capital, without the presence of the Caledonian and North Staffordshire, was £332,402,986. Throughout the document, the G&SWR is referred to as 'The Glasgow Company'.

Four Scottish seats out of twenty-three would hardly inspire confidence that interests north of the border would be, if not prominently considered, at least not forgotten about altogether. From the new company's point of view, it would soon become obvious that a strong third voice — as an alternative to the rival factions of Crewe and Derby — would have given the LMS greater stability, and might have resulted in a better locomotive policy being adopted from the start.

While it is true that the LNER only allocated five of the twenty-six seats in the boardroom to Scottish constituents, the fact that one was the chairman's was obviously a compensatory factor and, as Dr Hughes has pointed out in his history, the LNER tended to operate with less than the full twenty-six anyway.

The 'Caley' did not go down without a fight. Whether the challenge was worth the effort put into it is questionable, but the fact remains that the Caledonian was one of only two major railways (the other was the North Staffordshire) which remained independent after the Act became law on 1 January.

Despite disputing the terms of Amalgamation, the Caledonian was, however, prepared to accept £886,249 from the Government for, 'arrears of maintenance and renewals of ways and works', out of a total national disbursement of £25 million.

What its shareholders could not accept was that the company's own valuation at the Grouping should be based on the trading year 1913, ten years earlier. On the face of it, this was not an ungenerous calculation — most of the UK's railways enjoyed considerable prosperity until the outbreak of war. Clearly, the Caledonian did not believe itself to be one of them, since it happened to be paying a dividend of only 3.5 per cent in 1913, so this apparently reasonable offer was deemed unacceptable. The 'Caley' decided to take the matter before an Amalgamation Tribunal, as it had a legal right to do.

No expense was spared in preparing for this crunch meeting, scheduled for June 1923, the company retaining two distinguished legal advisers — Sir John Simon, a former Home Secretary, and Hugh Pattison Macmillan, soon to be Lord Advocate and, later, Baron Macmillan. In the meantime, 'all our principal officers have been appointed to the new organisation. We are glad to know that their merits have been recognised', the Caledonian informed *The Railway Times*. The company spokesman added that, in the meantime, the 'Caley' operated as part of the new Group. (Also, CR directors joined the LMS Scottish Local Committee from January, as described later.).

The Tribunal took a whole week in June 1923 to resolve the problem of valuation, despite the fact that the Government appeared to offer nothing new in its compensatory terms. Macmillan went as far as to describe the offer as '*cauld kail het agen*' (cold cabbage reheated!). Despite his verbosity, the Caledonian's appeal was disallowed; the company lost, and a formal notice was issued that its railway system would finally be absorbed on 1 July 1923. Some stockholders were driven to fury, *The Railway Times* quoting one of them as pointing out that these were, 'equivalent terms to those granted to the preferred ordinary stock of the G&SWR without going to the Tribunal at all!' It looks as if Granet had kept his promise!

Approved by Government from the start, its prospectus published at Westminster in 1844, the Caledonian Railway ended its existence in conflict with London, and all to no avail. It was a disappointingly negative end to a company which had been conceived so imaginatively, as an integral part of a national transport network. Planned with flair and operated with panache, it had earned the accolade of 'The' Caledonian (i.e. Scottish) Railway. Even if its title and aspirations may have bordered, particularly at first, on the grandiose, it grew into a magnificent concern. It deserved a better ending than this.

In addition to the major rail companies being assigned to one of four main groupings, a scattering of minor companies were wound up and incorporated into the 'Big Four'. The new LMS swallowed up twenty-seven subsidiaries throughout the UK, the LNER twenty-six. Two joint railways which escaped Grouping were the Prince's Dock Joint line at Greenock, and the Forth Bridge Railway. Both of these survived as separate entities until Nationalisation on 1 January 1948 (and will be discussed later).

The best known of the minor railways absorbed by the LMS were probably the Cathcart District Railway, and the Callander & Oban. The first of these is a 6-mile loop from a junction 1.5 miles out of Glasgow (Central), running through the city's southern suburbs back to Pollokshields.

Like so many extensions to the Caledonian network after 1860, the Cathcart District Railway was a 'proxy' railway. Researchers examining the company archives will find that the first meeting of the directors took place, not at Caledonian headquarters, but in a solicitor's office in West Regent Street on 16 December 1880. The area encircled by the line was by no means urbanised at that time, but the Caledonian knew a good investment when it saw one, and was anxious in any event to prevent G&SWR expansion in the area. Not surprisingly, the CR put up half the capital and operated the line at cost. At one time, there was a train every ten minutes on the circle, a frequency unequalled anywhere else outside London.

The CDR lasted until January 1923 as an independent company, being taken over by the LMS six months earlier than the Caledonian itself. In retrospect it is surprising that the new owners did not see electrification of a busy circle line as an obvious investment worth making, especially since this would have eradicated engine-changing on an intensively operated service. This did not happen until well into BR days – and after the electrification of the former NBR lines north of the Clyde.

The Callander & Oban was an independent concern right up to 1923, although always operated by the Caledonian. Its unique history has been well recorded by the late John Thomas (see Bibliography), and it still carries trains through the Pass of Brander, where North American-style double-arm semaphore signals can still be seen. The company's Ballachullish branch, built northwards from the C & O across the striking Connel Ferry Bridge, was legally a separate company and was absorbed by the LMS as a constituent in its own right.

Another short independent line running off the C & O was the Killin Railway. Opened in 1886, this 5-mile branch was also operated by the Caledonian, the 0-4-4 tank engines lasting on the line almost until closure in 1966. John Thomas has pointed out that when Amalgamation was formally proposed, the Killin company secretary, seeing 'Euston' on official correspondence, assumed that his little line was to be taken over by the London & North Western!

Among the minor concerns absorbed into the LMS was the Solway Junction Railway (of which more below, relating to the demolition of its viaduct). By the time the Railways Act of 1921 became law, the Solway company was being administered, in name only, from Sandown on the Isle of Wight, its grasp of detail being shown by the complete omission of any mention of the viaduct's closure in that year's company papers! Nevertheless, the usual bonanza was paid to the directors – and although in the case of SJR it only amounted to £150 among them, this was literally money for nothing.

A more northern subsidiary was the Dornoch Light Railway, connecting the county town of Sutherland with the Highland Far North line at The Mound. It is pleasing to record that this line, constructed for what one could describe as charitable reasons – to help the area's agriculture, tourism, and fishing industry to develop – nevertheless made a profit annually up until 1920, and even then was able to make good an £800 loss from carefully husbanded reserves. The line was operated by the Highland, who also opened the impressive Station Hotel. When wound up, the DLR, whose records can be read at the National Archives of Scotland in Edinburgh, had an unpaid dividend of £6 3s 6d to disburse, but the new LMS paid out

£350 in winding-up costs. £300 of this was paid to the company secretary as compensation for the loss of his employment, an infinitely preferable transaction to the usual payola made to company directors.

To complete the list of minor constituents of the LMS should be numbered the Arbroath & Forfar; Brechin & Edzell District; Dundee & Newtyle; Glasgow, Barrhead & Kilmarnock; Glasgow & Paisley; Lanarkshire & Ayrshire; Portpartick & Wigtownshire; and Wick & Lybster Light.

One of the first tasks of the new LMS Local Scottish Committee was to consider the retirement of the secretary of two of these lines – the Glasgow & Paisley, and the Glasgow Barrhead & Kilmarnock. The individual concerned was Mr James Ker, who also served in the same capacity for the Prince's Dock Joint Railway. The first two lines were being absorbed by the LMS anyway, but the third would continue as an independent entity, at least on paper, for another twenty-five years, and a new secretarial appointment would have to be made (see the chapter 'Joint Interests'). It appeared that Mr Ker had spent forty-two of his sixty-two years in the service of these 'paper' railways, but was not now in good health, and unfortunately was not a member of any superannuation scheme. In view of his good service, the LMS committee voted him a pension of £120 per annum. Within seven weeks, however, Mr Ker had passed on, and the committee decided to pay the current year's pension to his widow.

The LNER incorporated the following minor, or in some cases, superseded companies, none of which operated their own services: Edinburgh & Bathgate; Forth & Clyde Junction; Gifford & Garvald; Kilsyth & Bonnybridge; Lauder Light; and Newburgh & North Fife. Perhaps the most interesting of these was the Forth & Clyde Junction Railway, a company based on Stirling and which had constructed a line westwards to Balloch on Loch Lomond. Never a lucrative concern, the company had managed to resist a takeover from the Caledonian, but threw in its lot with the North British in 1866, when that company had just gained considerable mileage – not to mention prestige – by absorbing the Edinburgh & Glasgow, which the Caledonian had long been expected to do. (Interestingly, the Forth & Clyde *Canal* was operated by the Caledonian, and then by the LMS – see the chapter 'Off the Rails'.)

But the absorption of the Forth & Clyde Junction by the LNER was not entirely smooth, and this caused the latter company having to make a rare appearance in the summer of 1923 in front of the Amalgamation Tribunal, established to settle any complaints about compensation arrangements. It appeared that although Forth & Clyde shareholders had received a modest dividend annually, this was actually being paid by the North British, who operated the lines owned by the smaller company. That this fact was not widely understood by shareholders is suggested by a number of distressing letters in the relevant file in the National Archives. It appears that some shareholders discovered that they were now about to receive only approximately 10 per cent of the face value of their shares in the Forth & Clyde. Appeals to the LNER on behalf of these 'poor people', as they were repeatedly referred to by their fund managers, drew a reply from the LNER pointing out that the Amalgamation Tribunal had already decided that the compensation terms were adequate in the circumstances.

The F & C company directors did a little better, receiving a disbursement of £200 among them – not bad for administering a company which did not run its own trains and could not pay its own dividends.

2

New Managements for Old?

The vast transformation of Britain's railway companies – the 1923 Grouping – failed to make an immediate impact as far as railwaymen and the travelling public were concerned. Patrick Ransome-Wallis admitted in his memoirs that he half expected to see a North British Atlantic at Sheffield on New Year's morning of that momentous year! For Norman McKillop at Edinburgh's Haymarket depot, one of the first signs of the new regime was the delivery to the shed stores of a consignment of dungarees, none of which seemed to fit any of the men!

Looking at the two companies, organisational differences between east and west soon became obvious. While the Caledonian, the LMS's principal Scottish company, made no contribution to the setting-up of what became Britain's biggest transport operation, the two smaller concerns, the G&SWR and Highland absorbed by the new super-company, were successful in securing some devolution of administrative functions. The historian Peter Tatlow has suggested that the Northern Division (i.e. Scottish and Northern Irish areas):

> ... tended in some ways to conform least to LMS Standardisation policies and indeed possessed a unique management structure... posts without equivalents in England and Wales included Commercial Manager, Steamship Superintendent, Mechanical and Electrical Engineer and Civil Engineer.

Geoff Hughes sees the LMS in a rather different light, writing:

The LMS, in somewhat cavalier fashion, but having regard to the existence of strong pre-Grouping rivalries likely to continue after the amalgamation, decided at the outset on a firm policy of centralisation.

O.S. Nock would appear to agree with this latter opinion, his history of the Highland Railway including the comment that:

Although a divisional organization was set up on the LMS, with headquarters in Glasgow, all points of major policy came to be dictated from London.

Perhaps there *was* some potential for local initiative on the LMS if senior management wished to show it. One senior manager in the south, P.E. Garbutt, recorded that he could not recall 'any of the LMS hierarchy being much interested in long-distance visits to Scotland!'

The LMS's first chairman was Lord Lawrence – hardly a prominent figure in British transport history, despite having chaired the LNWR – and within two years he had been succeeded by Sir Guy Granet, whose prominence was undeniable. Granet had been chairman of the Midland and had served under Geddes both in military administration in the Great War, and on the Committee on National Expenditure in 1921/22. Perhaps his most positive contribution to LMS administration was to establish a 'vertical' structure for the company, creating the new post of president, with four vice-presidents reporting in four distinct technical and commercial areas – two dealing with traffic operating, and one each dealing with accounting and works. (The last of these posts went to R.W. Reid, a Midland man who was the son of the former NBR engineer responsible for that company's formidable 'Atlantics'.).

It was a reform that was nothing if not bold, and for the selection of the first president, Granet went 'outside the tribe', appointing Sir Josiah Stamp (later, Lord Stamp). The latter's biographical details are highly impressive – from a far-from-affluent home, forced to leave school early, self-taught to university standard. Stamp brought considerable business expertise to the LMS, mixed with the common sense that can only be acquired by leaving school at fifteen. However, from the point of view of the LMS in Scotland, it is noticeable that there was no direct Scottish element in all this; indeed O.S. Nock believed that 1926 saw the last of any pre-Grouping Scottish influence on the new company.

On the other hand, the LNER clearly believed in delegated powers, allowing local decision-making and a faster response to problems. The new company established three areas – Southern, North Eastern, and Scottish – from London northwards, each with its own general manager. There was an undoubted feeling of devolved powers, particularly when compared to what Dr Hughes calls: 'the omnipotence which Euston was said to have held over the LMS'. He suggests that senior LNER officials effectively promised their area management to settle policy and deal with the board, while 'you get on with running the railway'.

In the Scottish area – which would operate just over a quarter of the company's total route-miles – the NBR's James Calder was appointed as the first Scottish area general manager, although his actual title was General Manager (Scotland), an early example of devolutionary intent.

Calder was so much of a North British man that he had even contrived to be born on the company's property! Originating from Blackhall in West Lothian, Calder was educated at nearby Shotts and Hamilton, before entering the company's service in the West of Scotland. Just before the First World War he joined the general manager's department in Edinburgh, succeeding to the top post in March 1918. His appointment as LNER General Manager (Scotland) seemed an obvious progression for one who showed no interest in taking his talents southwards.

On paper, Calder's counterpart on the LMS was the divisional general superintendent, John Ballantyne. Beginning his career as a humble clerk at Beattock station in 1892, Ballantyne graduated up to Glasgow where he showed previously unsuspected managerial talent in reorganising the Accounts office, before taking the post of assistant, and then in 1918 chief goods manager. But the new LMS hedged its bets on its Scottish management and appointed a 'pro consul' with Ballantyne – Donald Alexander Matheson. The latter was an engineer born in Perthshire, but who learned his trade with rail contractors in England. On returning to his homeland, he worked on the Edinburgh South Suburban railway (an NBR company) before making a name for himself on the Caledonian's Central underground line. The 'Caley' asked him to join the fold, and by 1899 he was the company's engineer-in-chief. His eminence was recognised in his being invited to join the Railway Executive Committee during the war, and in acting as an advisor to the Ministry of Transport.

If it appears that the appointment of these two Caledonian employees – with Matheson as divisional manager (Scotland) being nominally higher than Ballantyne who was entitled general superintendent, Northern Division – was the result of the new parent company being unable to make up its mind between two highly respected company servants, the puzzle is compounded by the fact that, when the LMS was being established, the Caledonian Railway had not even consented to join!

Besides being represented on the board of the LMS – perhaps under-represented would be more accurate – the three Scottish constituents of the new LMS were asked to supply nominees to a Scottish Local Committee. This body was formally instituted at an LMS board meeting at Euston on 15 December 1922, with the motion being proposed by chairman Lawrence, and seconded by vice-chairman Granet. As a consequence, the first meeting of the new committee convened at St Enoch Station twelve days later.

Not surprisingly, the committee members present (Charles Ker, Sir Archibald Garvie, and David Cooper, from the G&SWR and Messrs Pullar and Wilson from the Highland) spent much of their time discussing what they were supposed to do! They had been given no detailed remit, and no information about how much spending power they might have. Nor were they able to finalise the chairmanship, as they were sensible enough to real-ise that they would have to wait for the Caledonian to resolve its differences with the Amalgamation Tribunal. Curiously, their wait was shorter than they might have expected – as we know, the Tribunal did not meet until June 1923 – but as early as mid-January the Caledonian sent along a number of directors, with the CR chairman, Henry Allan, accepting the invitation to chair the Local Committee. He held this post only until the beginning of July, when he resigned as the last chairman of the Caledonian.

While this new committee may have been regarded by some as a 'second-division' board of directors, and has not figured largely in the popular histories of the LMS, it nevertheless was a useful tool for unifying the Scottish mem-bers of the company as far as possible, and may well explain the dominance of the Caledonian in operational matters right from the start, when in theory that company was still independent. However, some of its earliest work per-tained to marine matters, in particular, how to timetable Loch Fyne steamers to avoid Admiralty torpedo firings! (See chapter 'Off the Rails'.).

The LNER also established a Scottish local area committee, its initial title being the Local Board Scottish Area. Its *raison d'être* is a puzzle to the trans-port historian, in view of the new company's establishment of a devolved management structure, one which fairly accurately represented the pre-1923 rail network in both Scotland and north-east England. (The gathering of former GNR, GER, and GCR main lines into the Southern area was perhaps less satisfactory.).

The historian is not the only one puzzled by the existence of this board – so were its members, it seems! The first meeting took place in Aberdeen on 8 February 1923 with William Whitelaw in the chair, and was attended by Messrs McCosh, Duffus, Gray and Murray. No staff members were named in the sederunt. As with the corresponding LMS board, there was much discussion on the board's remits and spending limits; these included local transport matters, hotels, estates below a certain value and engineering works up to £1,000 (non-capital), as well as matters specially remitted to the Local board. Those present decided they also wished to cover cartage, motor vehicles, retirement allowances and the appointment of station masters up to an annual salary of £500.

The board's Minutes were handwritten well into the 1930s. On the other hand, all management communications to be found in the National Archives, are typed. It is difficult to avoid the conclusion that the Local Area board was of marginal importance – established only to pre-empt any nationalistic outrage at the loss of local control in 1923. The fact that Whitelaw and his colleagues spent a major part of that first meeting discussing purchases for the wine list at the Aberdeen Palace Hotel confirms that the LNER really was letting professional railwaymen get on with running the railway!

The territory of the two constituent companies of the LNER in Scotland was recognised with the establishment of the Southern Scottish Area, comprising the former NBR system, and the Northern, which of course covered the former GNSR. Before the decade was out, however, there was a move to eliminate the Northern Scottish division, which was, in some ways, too small a unit to stand comparison with the Southern Scottish. From the outset, the division had been denied a divisional general manager, and the Audit and General Accounts offices were transferred to Edinburgh within the year.

The GNSR's general manager, George Davidson, was moved sideways into a legal advisory role, where no doubt he missed having his salary being paid free of income tax, which the GNSR had done! Unusually, Davidson went on to become general manager of the North Eastern Area in 1924, holding the post until his death four years later. William Johnston effectively ran the new division under the title of traffic superintendent – previously he had done so as GNSR superintendent of the line since 1918, having begun his company service as a 'boy clerk'.

Michael Bonavia believes the resistance to eliminating the separate Northern Division was headed by director A.R. Gray (originally an NBR Director) and supported by chairman Whitelaw. Obviously, the old GNSR system was well-thought of in the boardroom! Incidentally, the former Great North boardroom in Aberdeen's Guild Street was regarded as the second largest and most handsomely appointed of all those accumulated by the new LNER. It was listed as the venue for meetings of the Aberdeen Joint Station Committee, certainly early in the working lives of the 'Big Two'.

As far as the public was concerned, appearances were going to be of paramount importance in the first year of the new companies' existence. Liveries, advertisements and uniforms would all be essential in setting a 'house style' and representing a united front, not just to the public, but to the widely scattered staff as well.

The LNER conducted at least two 'fashion shows' featuring locomotives, one exhibiting existing liveries at York on 31 January, and a later event showing possible new locomotive liveries at Marylebone on 22 February. After the first of these, the *North Eastern Magazine*, not yet elevated to full LNER magazine status (see below), was handsome enough to declare the North British representative, 'a more impressive engine to the layman than any of the others'. This was Atlantic No.874 *Dunedin*, whose company livery was described as 'bronze green' (the exact shade had been a source of comment in Scotland for decades). However, by the time of the Marylebone event, sister engine No.876 *Waverley* had been decked out in apple-green with black and white lining and vermilion motion. It was not long before this became standard for passenger locomotives on the LNER, (apart from the vermilion) and adverse comment is missing from contemporary documents – in other words, Scottish staff and passengers were probably happy to be rid of the 'bronze'! In his enjoyable book *The Springburn Story*, the historian John Thomas opines that the NBR Scott 4-4-0s 'never looked more handsome' than in LNER green.

Over on the LMS only one colour seemed to be considered. It was a lovely colour too – the Midland's 'crimson lake' – but to apply it universally, so soon, seemed a tad insensitive. (The choice of a livery not used by any of the principal lines would have been diplomatic.). LNWR painters were reported to be have refused to apply 'crimson lake' to their beloved 'Claughtons', while the painting over of 'Caledonian blue' must have caused a few ructions at St Rollox; 'we nearly came out on strike', an elderly painter told John Thomas. Perhaps not surprisingly, a former Caledonian 4-4-0, No.1081, was still running in CR livery, complete with original numberplates, in 1931 – eight years after Grouping!

Both new companies sought armorial distinction. The LNER's crest was the larger and more imposing, its centrepiece being the motto 'Forward', inherited from the Great Central Railway. Scottish thistles were featured, along with Edinburgh Castle making up one-quarter of a central shield device. Only two locomotives are believed to have carried this crest – one of them the legendary Pacific, *Flying Scotsman*, when on display at the Wembley Exhibition of 1924 – and the LNER was soon to turn to Eric Gill's calligraphic skills to represent it throughout most of its twenty-five-year existence.

The LMS used its crest almost ubiquitously on its carriage stock, but it was perhaps a less effective emblem; indeed, heraldic authority George Dow called it 'uninspiring'. Although English and Scottish symbols (roses and thistles) were featured, one expert has pointed out that the crest failed to indicate that, of the four new grouped railways, the LMS was unique in supplying rail services to England, Scotland, Wales and Northern Ireland.

Both of the new companies hoped to give their enormous workforces a sense of 'togetherness' by publishing staff magazines. They set about it in different ways, the LMS creating a brand-new publication, while the LNER gradually elevated the former North Eastern Railway organ to take on all-line status.

In January 1923, the *North Eastern Railway Magazine* was already in its 13th volume, disseminating news on company matters, appointments, retirements and deaths, as well as items on sport, allotments and humorous articles in an (to this author) unidentifiable dialect which could presumably be understood from Yorkshire to the Tweed.

Nevertheless, the editor used plain English in commenting upon news-paper reaction to the launch of the 'Big Four' companies, suggesting that they were, 'giving to it perhaps .0001% of the space they sometimes devote to a really interesting murder'.

The LNER obviously felt that this very professional publication should become the basis for a new overall magazine, although the transformation was gradual, and even by the end of 1924 it was styled the *North Eastern and Scottish Magazine (LNER)*, the July issue of that year carrying morale-boosting messages from Sir Ralph Wedgwood, James Calder, and Alex Wilson, the DGM from the North Eastern Area.

The LMS, on the other hand, decided to start from scratch. Mindful that it was the largest single employer in the UK, it commissioned the *LMS Railway Magazine*, although the first issue did not appear until November of that first year, distributed by 500 staff members, and carrying an appeal for more volunteers to improve the distribution level. It was fairly dreary stuff, opening with a morale-boosting message from general manager Arthur Watson, and issuing uninteresting statistics about financial matters.

One concession to the widespread nature of the company was to include four-page sections for each of four areas, the Northern Division having its page numbers preceded by 'D', for 'all stations north of, and excluding, Carlisle'. Presumably, four different editions were produced, but the library copies this author has studied have pagination continued through sections A–D. No Irish material appeared to be included. Perhaps a bibliographical historian can clarify all this in the fullness of time!

In the first issue we learn that the 'young ladies of the Divisional Goods Managers staff in Glasgow intend running a small whist drive and dance early this month', and there was a picture of Glasgow-based apprentices on a picnic outing. More interesting was a report of the award of a silver cup to trace boy Wilson K. Elder, for his care and management of his horse, 'a handsome grey Percheron'. It was an indicator of the times that no explanation of 'trace' was thought necessary. It probably is nowadays: a trace horse assisted a draughthorse to haul a cart or lorry up a steep hill, and this particular animal worked on Glasgow's West Nile Street, 'to the admiration of passing pedestrians'. The Caledonian had purchased the animal when it was brought to London after the First World War, 'numerous signs of which it still bears on its body'. Elder received a cup from the Glasgow and West of Scotland SPCA, and was personally commended by Arthur Watson in the next issue. It was a world away from the modern transport scene, but a pleasant detail from a forgotten time.

Two operational matters, one LMS and the other LNE, will now be examined as case histories to see to what extent the differing management arrangements manifested themselves during the resolution of administrative problems. Both relate to matters in the south of Scotland, one on the Solway, the other near the Tweed.

The demolition of the Solway Viaduct has already been related in detail by this author in another work, but is worth looking at in relation to the extent where everyday decisions were beyond the remit of the local, or more exactly divisional, LMS officials. This involved nothing apparently more serious than the wording of an advert having to be approved by London, but the consequent delay had major, even fatal, consequences. The decision to close the Solway Junction Railway's central section – the 1,900-yard viaduct which crossed the silver estuary of the Solway – had already been taken by the Caledonian before Grouping, and with no great reluctance.

That company had only supported the independent backers of the SJR in order to ensure that no other company drove a bridgehead into the Gretna–Beattock corridor, which provided the 'Caley' with a natural route north from Carlisle. Nor would they have wanted to see another Scottish company penetrating deeper down the north-west coast of England. Not only was the G&SWR interested in the operations of the Cumberland-backed SJR, the North British was active in offering a deal to the Cumbrian ironmasters building into Scotland. At one time the likelihood of a NBR connection was so real (and they already had a physical one to the SJR from their Silloth branch) that Annan Shawhill Station was slated for NBR staffing. Not only that, but the SJR/G&SWR Junction, just east of the latter company's Annan Station, was listed in an 1865 parliamentary document as an exchange point for traffic between these two allies, the NBR and G&SWR – allied, of course, against the Caledonian, with whom the G&SWR became a reluctant partner following the Grouping.

So there was no possibility of the new LMS attempting to resurrect the cross-Solway route by undertaking the repairs necessary on the rotting structure in 1923. Quite the contrary; in the early 1930s the new company showed a casual, indeed unprofessional, attitude to its responsibilities in the dismantling of the viaduct. At one stage of the bungled demolition, company officials authorised the use of explosives – in an estuary where whole communities were dependent on fisheries for a living.

At that time, no senior LMS staff had bothered to leave Glasgow to visit the site for themselves, nor had they troubled to discuss the demolition with the Board of Trade, regarding the hazards this might cause seafarers. The problem centred on the LMS failing to specify whether, and how, dismantling should take place below high-water level, and this was obviously a matter of more than academic interest to those who make their living from the sea, particularly when it appeared that a series of artificial reefs had formed round the viaduct's piers.

This mismanagement could have emanated from any badly run company, but the point of specifying this episode in examining the LMS's structure within Scotland concerns the fact that the posters advertising demolition of the viaduct had to be approved by Euston! Newspaper advertisements also had to have the seal of approval from company headquarters, and this resulted in a delay in engaging a contractor. The latter was then forced to work against the clock in 1934, with nearly a month of summer weather being lost, and this, on the unpredictable Solway Firth, was no minor matter. Three workmen who died during the demolition appeared to have lost their lives when working from a boat which capsized, and it is difficult to separate all this from the pressure forced on the contractors by the inefficiency of the LMS.

It would simply not have happened on the LNER, where decision-making on such matters would have gone no higher than the area general manager, based in Edinburgh, and probably not even as high as that. But the LNER's division into three areas was not without its faults, and these were exposed at Kelso, in the valley of that other border waterway, the Tweed, only three years after Grouping.

In 1926, the decision to hold the Royal Highland Show at Kelso gave the LNER a logistical challenge of major proportions – and this only a few hundred yards away from the 'frontier' between the Scottish and North Eastern Areas. (The show is, of course, permanently based at Ingliston, near Edinburgh, nowadays, although it will be forced to move again if airport extension goes ahead nearby.).

When it is considered that the 1925 show had attracted 58,000 spectators, and Kelso Station had only one ladies' toilet, an idea can be gained of the problems the LNER was facing! Passenger capacity was only one aspect – the goods facilities would have to be able to load, and unload, up to 500 wagons of livestock and agricultural equipment overnight before and after the two-day show. So modest were the Kelso facilities – where the goods yard sidings were so curved as to necessitate the use of horses – that the LNER's area superintendent, Maj. Stemp, recommended against the choice of Kelso as an exhibition venue at all.

This was an 'own goal' of massive proportions. The show had not visited Kelso since 1898, when the NBR was reported to have coped satisfactorily (but with what was certainly a smaller event), and local councillors were quick to accuse the LNER of prejudice against the area. In an example of good public relations, the company's chairman, William Whitelaw no less, moved swiftly to assure the agricultural community that the LNER was not trying to dictate farming policy in the area. Privately, he told the Scottish Area staff: 'The thing wants careful handling'.

The LNER had estimated that £1,500 would have to be spent on temporary facilities, principally a loading bay on a running line (and on a 1 in 75 gradient). In the event, the work was done for less than half that amount. Archival papers give no hint as to whether the railway sought any kind of compensation or guarantees to cover for this, but the new loading bank became a permanent fixture.

The number of livestock wagons processed during the show came to 295, all of them despatched by 3.15 on the morning after the event. There were 752 wagon loads of equipment handled – twice – and all this within a five-day period, and 11,407 passenger tickets were sold, with a turnover of £5,267 7s 3d. These were, of course, for double journeys, meaning that around 5,500 people had travelled by rail. Overall attendance was approximately 49,000, showing that, even as early as the mid-1920s, the railway company was losing traffic to road. Indeed, one local transport concern had boasted to the border newspapers that it would put forty buses on the road to cater for show traffic.

An unforeseen complication was a royal presence at the show, the Prince of Wales arriving at Berwick on an overnight train. He was sent on to Kelso by special. This was typical of the work of the company's North Eastern Area, whose managers provided sterling assistance to their Scottish colleagues. Offers were made to take train rakes for storage east of Sprouston whenever required, and all locomotives on westbound trips were watered before entering the Kelso area. Weather conditions on the final day posed an additional problem – flash-flooding covered the line above rail height at one time.

The excellent liaison between Scottish and North Eastern Area staff was in fact the exact *opposite* of the usual arrangements on this cross-border line. Normally, the two areas behaved as if they were two separate companies, with no advertised connections at Kelso. Indeed, the North East area timetables indicated that the line from Tweedmouth actually stopped at Kelso! It was a major criticism of the new LNER of taking administrative devolution to the point of partisanship – particularly when railwaymen at grass-roots level had shown themselves only too happy to work together on common traffic problems.

One positive aspect to emerge from this 1926 episode to distinguish the higher levels of LNER management, was that the chairman was prepared to involve himself in the 'bread and butter' aspects of company business, and this could have positive long-term effects, making it clear to ordinary railwaymen that their bosses' boss might turn up in their office or on their footplate any day!

Much of the above activity at Kelso took place in May 1926 – a time without parallel in British industrial history, and an unhappy blemish on Scotland's. The LNER bore the brunt of it.

3

The General Strike

If there is any aspect of British railway history – indeed, British social history – that is best told from the point of view of the LMS and LNER in Scotland, it is the story of the General Strike of 1926.

This was a unique episode in transport history when the companies invited members of the public to drive and fire railway locomotives, or control traffic movements from lineside signalboxes. Not surprisingly, three members of the Scottish public lost their lives travelling by train, and it is a miracle the death-toll was no higher as untrained volunteers wrestled with the complexities of operating a national railway service. Their incompetence was not helped by the violence and sabotage mounted during that ill-fated week.

For many years, the standard work on this unhappy event was *The General Strike* by Julian Symons, in which we read that, 'indignation against the volunteers was strong, but not often carried to the point of violence'. A similar comment – and a contemporary one – came from the *Railway Gazette*, which opined that the '... small amount of attempted violence on the part of the strikers [was one of] the outstanding features of the strike period'.

This would have come as news to the LMS and LNER managements in Scotland. These English-based comments make it quite clear that Scotland bore the brunt of the confrontation. For, writing to James Calder, LNER chairman William Whitelaw wired, not long after the end of the strike: 'You must all have had a bad time carrying on amidst all the violence of the Miners in Scotland. We all realized your difficulties and are grateful to you all for the way you overcame them'.

Calder was pleased with this, and the company records (now in the National Archives of Scotland) show that he immediately had this message copied to heads of departments. One of them responded gloomily, 'The Chairman's comments would have given me considerable pleasure if I had been able to agree that it was only the "violence of the miners" we had to contend with. The riotous conduct and blackguardism of the Railwaymen, or a certain section of them, was only too apparent'.

Few people alive today can remember the General Strike, so a resumé of this violent episode is necessary. (Incidentally, the author's late mother was temporarily laid off – unpaid – from her clerical position with a boiler-making firm, as they were unable to bring in coal for their furnace and move out finished products.). It was an ordeal which touched almost every working person.

The conflict began in the coalfields, when the industries' owners attempted to protect their profits at a time of recession by forcing a wage cut on their workforce. Since the miners were only interested in making a living, not a profit, they naturally resented the loss of negotiated rates, and appealed for support in strike action. A Triple Alliance had been formed some years earlier among the miners, railwaymen and other transport workers to ensure that combined strike action could be brought to bear against what was seen as a hostile ruling class. Effectively, the rail unions' involvement in the General Strike was what we would now recognise as a 'secondary' dispute, and it has to be said that only a few years had passed since the footplatemen had secured an eight-hour day for themselves, and a standardisation of employment conditions nationally. (Incidentally, the pre-Grouping companies had argued against the application of a UK standard in employment conditions. They were routed by the arguments of James Thomas, a former GWR railwayman who later became a cabinet minister.).

Ranged against the Triple Alliance was a government, seen by many historians as right wing, and prepared to overcome any industrial unrest without concession. Civil Commissioners were appointed for particular areas, with an Organisation for the Maintenance of Supplies established. This was intended to recruit, and maintain a register of, volunteer labour, but only one of five categories of recruit was required to have technical knowledge of rail operation, the four grouped railways being expected to recruit their own volunteers from among retired railway staff, students and, no doubt, knowledgeable railway enthusiasts.

It is difficult to believe that the authorities, and particularly the railway companies, believed that they could operate any semblance of a public service in the event of a major stoppage. More probably, they believed they would never have to, so much so that, when the strike call was made late on 3 May 1926, the companies were astonished at the railwaymen's response.

Britain awoke to a silent landscape on Tuesday 4 May 1926. There was no rattle of trams on city streets, and no roar of factory or furnace. On the rails, the strike response was almost complete.

Of 440 people employed at Edinburgh (Waverley), only the stationmaster and one assistant reported. At Glasgow (Central), the stationmaster recorded the names of only four other senior staff in his strike diary. The LNER could move only one train in every thirty scheduled in the UK as a whole, with the proportion even lower on the company's Scottish lines. Even the LNER ferries across the Forth were affected, at Queensferry and between Granton and Burntisland, although both served road vehicles. On the LMS, only 207 drivers reported for work out of a total of more than 15,000 in the UK, and only 153 guards out of 9,979. Fewer than 900 signalling staff reported, out of 12,000, and 82 shunters out of 7,671.

At Glasgow (Central) only two trains worked in on that Tuesday morning, the first of them at 1.40 a.m. – a combined train from Aberdeen, Dundee, and Edinburgh, sent northwards from Carstairs instead of being allowed to proceed to Carlisle. The Edinburgh passengers were recorded as being particularly bitter at finding themselves in Glasgow. Well they might. The myth of the 'Red Clyde' seemed real enough at the time, and trouble was anticipated there. The Government-sponsored newspapers made great play on the Admiralty despatching a cruiser, HMS *Corus*, up the Clyde and into Glasgow, while two capital warships, the *Hood* and the *Warspite*, stood off the Tail o' the Bank below Greenock. In the city itself on that day, sixty-six strikers were arrested after police baton-charged a demonstration. Edinburgh was little better, with a mounted policeman suffering a fractured skull when his horse was allegedly stampeded by demonstrators.

Only five trains worked out of Central on 4 May, the 1.30 p.m. being the only one to essay the route to England. Lockerbie was recorded as its destination as it left, crewed by driver David Gibson, the star of two 'non-stop' escapades within the next three years, and a 'student fireman'. All the low-level traffic was stopped, and Central, probably the busiest station in Britain outside London in normal times, could only muster seven trains in and out on the whole of the next day. On 6–7 May 1926, this traffic had grown to ten trains each way, but a heavy price was being paid. The Edinburgh trains travelling through the Lanarkshire coalfield were targeted with stones continuously, the 3.50 p.m. arrival on 11 May 1926 arriving with a woman passenger injured by flying glass.

When one reads Patrick Renshaw's statement in an otherwise authoritative history of the General Strike, that, on the first day of the stoppage, 'a train ran from the North of England to the south, stopping at every station on a circuitous route', it hardly needs emphasising that historians have missed a major source of conflict through their usual casual treatment of the railways – Britain's greatest industry at the time.

One train which attempted to make its way to the south from Edinburgh Waverley on 10 May – and met with a serious case of sabotage – was the 'Flying Scotsman'. This service had proved impossible to operate in the strike's first three days, but by 7 May 1926 a train was dispatched from Waverley. As it departed with 180 passengers, Calder refused to hazard a possible arrival time at King's Cross, wiring London 'cannot say when it will arrive London, certainly not before tomorrow'. This train did arrive safely, which is more than can be said for the 'Scotsman', which left Waverley three days later with 100 more passengers.

One of the worst cases of violence was the derailment at Cramlington, Northumberland, for which eight men, described as colliers, received sentences of between four and eight years' penal servitude at Newcastle Assizes on 1 July 1926. The later MoT enquiry learned that a permanent way patrol had been chased by a stone-throwing mob before taking refuge at Cramlington Station. From here, it was possible to warn the oncoming express of possible danger ahead, but even this was insufficient to prevent No.2565 *Merry Hampton* toppling onto her side, taking five of her twelve coaches with her. Thankfully, there were no fatalities, but the volunteer fireman was reportedly scalded, and at least one passenger was injured.

There was some controversy later as to whether a rail on the down line had been physically removed, or merely loosened within its chairs. The MoT inspector appeared to favour the former theory, despite the claim of the four footplatemen, two of them regulars, that they had an uninterrupted view of the line ahead.

One of those convicted was William Muckle, who published his memories of the incident fifty-five years later. Muckle had begun colliery work at the age of thirteen for 10*d* for a ten-hour day, and his bitterness about the social and working conditions which he and those around him suffered, remained with him to the end of his life. According to his autobiography, *No regrets*, Muckle was among the twenty to twenty-five who physically removed a rail on the East Coast main line, being particularly angry that he was one of eight who was imprisoned, following the testimony of colleagues who turned King's Evidence. Muckle later argued that eight men would have been insufficient to physically manhandle a rail, and that the Crown was transparently buying prosecution evidence from those who were as culpable as he.

The decision to 'have a rail up' was made immediately after a meeting at the Cramlington Miners' Institute on the morning of 10 May 1926. Muckle implies that he made this call, his intention being, 'to stop the blackleg coal trains going through'. With three colleagues, he broke into a platelayers hut on the nearby ECML, to obtain necessary tools, and after the midday meal, 'we took the rail up in record time'. They then chased a volunteer permanent-way gang, reputedly dressed in 'plus fours'. (This was very much an often-repeated and derisive description of the image of the volunteer, as seen by the striker.). According to the volunteers' account, two of their number were injured in this incident, but they succeeded in warning the southbound 'Flying Scotsman' by stopping it north of Cramlington Station.

What happened then is, in retrospect, surprising. The train restarted almost immediately, its crew later stating that they were under the impression that they were being warned only about stone-throwing ahead, something they had already endured in the coal-mining vicinity of Prestonpans. Muckle wrote:

> The only thing I was sorry about was that the train we tipped was 'The Flying Scotsman' with 281 people on board. I say now we were thankful there was nobody killed (just one man had his foot hurt), but when you come to think again it was a General Strike and they were blacklegs running the trains ... In the final analysis they could have stopped it (the 'Scotsman') but they did not. They were given plenty of warning.

As in other incidents (Bishop's Stortford in England, St Margaret's in Scotland), the decision-making by professional railwaymen, or their management, can only be seen as error-ridden. Here, a locomotive crew was prepared to press on without fully acquainting themselves of the nature of the problem ahead. The evidence at the MoT enquiry shows that, at the very least, the PW gang were aware that a lineside hut containing tools had been broken into, and it is difficult to understand how the real nature of the problem ahead was not sufficiently grasped by the crew. Possibly, it was an unconscious thought process; the regular drivers (of whom there were two on the footplate, a Haymarket man and a conductor/driver taken on at Berwick) believing that they had to remain calm in the face of the amateurs' concern? It was almost certain that the engine-driver was not from one of the upper 'links' at Haymarket if he was not familiar with the line south of Berwick, and he may not have been very experienced.

After short periods in Durham, Leeds, and Pentonville, Muckle was incarcerated in Maidstone prison, being released after twenty-seven months, the other saboteurs also having their sentences reduced to no more than forty-two months. Unlike some of his colleagues, Muckle seemed to have withstood imprisonment stoically. Asked by one of them, 'Do you think we'll ever get out of this place?', Muckle had replied, 'What do you want to get out for?' – a telling comment on how many a miner must have viewed his existence at that time.

Ironically, when being taken through Leeds Central Station as one of four chained and handcuffed prisoners, Muckle caught a glimpse of a nearby locomotive. It was *Merry Hampton*.

A cabinet paper of the time suggested that two armoured cars, one on the road, the other rail-mounted, should patrol within 27 miles north and south of Newcastle during any future dispute, but it was in Scotland where there were no fewer than six cases of sabotage. These included interference with the permanent way at Newcraighall on Edinburgh's eastern outskirts, and at two locations in Fife. At Newcraighall, signalling wires were broken on 7 May 1926, a wagon (presumably stationary) derailed, lineside battery boxes broken into, and heaps of stones piled upon two running lines. Fishplates and keys were removed from the up line between Thornton and Cardenden, and a potential site for a derailment created in the early hours of 11 May – fortunately found by an inspection patrol – and a loose piece of rail wedged into points at Cowdenbeath South Junction. This last obstacle was not cleared until the 15th of the month. A pair of wheels from a plate-layer's bogie was sent rolling down an incline near Cardenden on the 8th, again, fortunately, without causing injury or damage, but a more potentially dangerous series of incidents bedevilled the 1255 Edinburgh (Waverley) – Anstruther passenger train on 7 May 1926.

When arriving at Burnhill, near Leven, the train crew found that level-crossing gates were secured against the train, and the presence of the police was necessary to have them opened. Nor was the train able to continue uneventfully, being diverted on to the Lochty branch at East Fife Central Junction, 'by the action of some evil disposed person or persons'. This probably involved unauthorised entry into a signalbox, and police again had to attend while the train reversed out of the branch. Ten railway staff were later fined following this incident, with the alternative of twenty days' imprisonment.

There was also a case of an LNER signalman interfering with a Westinghouse brake at Banchory on the Deeside line; an incident which resulted in dismissal and a £30 fine, with the alternative of sixty days' imprisonment. This appears to have been the only recorded case of sabotage directed against rolling stock by railway staff.

Interestingly, Angela Tucket has pointed out (in Jeffrey Skelley's *The General Strike*) that there was no recorded case whatever of sabotage against locomotives, adding 'there was no need, for the inexperienced volunteers on the footplate themselves did massive damage'. In her absorbing essay on the history of the strike in Swindon, she comments intuitively, 'no railwayman, of course, would cause wilful damage to his beloved friend and enemy, the engine'.

Considering the level of resentment against strike-breaking, this was a surprisingly low level of damage inflicted on the rail system, particularly in view of the number of (non-railway staff) strikers who took up position beside the tracks armed with stones.

Throwing stones at moving trains cannot be seen as anything short of vandalism, and very dangerous vandalism at that, although there is evidence that missile-throwing strikers were not all as murderous as those recorded near Newcastle or in Glasgow. The wife of a Swindon railwayman was recorded as taking up a daily position beside the Great Western Railway lines to throw stones at moving trains as an expression of her defiance and anger at strike-breaking. This was far removed from the epidemic of missile-throwing which forced an LNER manager to record, 'As far as our railway experience went... the Mob ruled in Glasgow and the West'. It is even further removed from the London-based historians' view of the General Strike as largely peaceable.

Time and again the records show trains arriving at their destinations with carriage glass smashed, while signalboxes were rendered useless, and volunteer platemen pelted with ballast. Even Julian Symons, in his somewhat anodyne account of rail operations conducted in the teeth of strikers' opposition, is forced to record the fate of a LNER train from Morpeth, consisting of a locomotive and a single coach traversing the coal-mining area to Newcastle, with not a window left on one side of the carriage on arrival. The three passengers were unhurt, one of them having lain full-length in the luggage rack with his coat over his head.

Not every stone-thrower's target was so lucky, however, particularly north of the border. Missile-throwing was so bad in Glasgow that on 9 May 1926, the LNER had to inform the District Civil Commissioner, Sir Arthur Rose, that it was no longer able to operate freight traffic in the city, owing to injuries already received (four men injured up to that date) and, 'the menacing attitude of the mobs' at different points:

Trainmen absolutely refuse to work to the Goods Depots at Sighthill, High Street, Bellgrove or Queen Street, and neither will they longer take their engines to and from Eastfield and Cowlairs or into Cadder Yard unless they can be assured... protection.

The worst incident happened at Petershill Bridge, when unknown assailants dropped a heavy coping-stone onto a locomotive passing underneath. This penetrated a tarpaulin which the driver had rigged up between cab and tender, but missed the crew by inches. When the LNER had to abandon the Cowlairs West signalbox on police advice, every pane of glass in the cabin was smashed, so the LNER called it a day, made their report to the Civil Commissioner, and then complained to the Lord Advocate, Scotland's principal law officer in the government, about their, 'failure to obtain proper military or police protection'.

There may have been two sides to this story of civil authority, being markedly unsympathetic to the railway's need for protection. Four days earlier, Sir Arthur Rose had asked the rail companies represented on his committee, to continue paying wages to strikers, in order to prevent civil disorder caused by genuine hardship. After refusing this request, all four companies met in London with two members of the Cabinet, and confirmed this refusal. It may have seemed logical in principle, but it may explain why the LNER received less protection than it deemed necessary.

In the circumstances, it is easy to see why the figures for Scottish freight traffic on the move dropped from 3.7 per cent to 0.4 per cent of normal workings (from thirty-four down to one) between the first and second days of the strike.

An exception to the bombarding of transport facilities with stones comes from the late John Thomas, Scotland's leading rail historian. Mr Thomas recalled in his book, *The Springburn Story*, a volunteer-driven tram being bombarded with bags of flour. He points out that road-mending materials were lying nearby, and could have been used to mortal effect, but local people preferred to buy flour from the local greengrocer's in order to make their point.

Britain's most serious rail accident during the strike occurred at St Margaret's in Edinburgh, but could not blamed on either sabotage or vandalism. At St Margaret's, running sheds and workshops straddled the main line at a site where thirty-three engines were built in NBR days. It was a lugubrious location, home to more than 200 steam locomotives, their exhausts a perennial source of pollution to nearby tenements.

On Monday 10 May 1926, at 3.05 p.m., only ten minutes after a fatal incident on the LNER at Bishop's Stortford, the 1.06 p.m. Berwick–Edinburgh (Waverley) passenger train was approaching St Margaret's, headed by 4-4-2 tank No.9450 working bunker-first. Unfortunately, it ran straight into a line of wagons on the main line, awaiting shunting into the depot on the down side. Three passengers were killed and eight injured, with eight more affected by gas escaping from the wrecked carriages within the short tunnel under the A1 road. Soldiers searching among the wreckage, which piled up to the tunnel ceiling, were forced to wear gas masks.

The Ministry of Transport lost no time in setting up an Inquiry, which met two days later under the chairmanship of Sir John Pringle. He concluded that the accident had been the product, firstly, of 'abnormal conditions', and secondly, by the failure of the Portobello signalman, a volunteer named Green, 'to obtain acceptance for the passenger train, and of R.A. Smeddle, assistant works manager at Cowlairs [who was driving]… to exercise the caution necessary to enable him to observe and obey hand signals'. An inspector working in St Margaret's Box was also blamed for not informing Green of the presence of the wagons, but Pringle concluded that: 'mistakes, failures or errors of judgment which were made in this unfortunate case are not unlike those made in past years by trained railwaymen in normal conditions, from which accidents have resulted'.

One is tempted to agree more with Pringle's first conclusion above – the 'abnormal conditions' – than with his second. The lack of normal signalling safeguards would appear to be the kernel of the problem, not least because Portobello West signalbox was some 1.5 miles away, with no fewer than three signalboxes nearer to the shunting train. Two of these boxes were unmanned at the time, but it is difficult to imagine the accident happening if they had been crewed, even by volunteers.

Pringle was soon forced to issue a supplementary report, having originally accepted evidence from the LNER that one of the intermediate boxes could not have its telegraph circuits switched out, something that was later proved to be incorrect – if switched out, the new extended section would not have had to be controlled by telephone only. Complicating the equation was the fact that one of these abandoned boxes had left its signals at danger, while the other – unfortunately the one nearer the unprotected train – had left them 'off'.

A later twist in the tale was the rail management's very serious allegation that striking railwaymen had failed to answer an appeal to help free injured passengers from the debris, a charge subsequently refuted after being raised in the House of Commons.

Not surprisingly, one of the injured survivors of the crash decided to sue the LNER for damages in the Court of Session. In the circumstances, it was astonishing that more of the injured, or the families of the dead, did not do the same, but what is even more surprising is that the company decided to defend the case. The LNER file shows their lawyers' unease at offering a defence, at a time when travelling conditions were 'notorious' (the LNER's exact description), and this is compounded by the fact that the plaintiff, Thomas Millar, was employed by Messrs Slaughter, the advertising agents whose signs were to be seen on every LNER station, certainly in the Edinburgh area – effectively an important customer.

The rail company's principal defence was that Mr Millar was travelling on a free pass supplied by his employers, and this pass carried a disclaimer saying that the passenger travelled at their own risk. But the defence lawyers could not have expected to get away with this; it was never going to override the company's obligation to provide its customers with a reasonably safe journey. Since their employee, the driver of No.9450, had admitted passing a signal at danger, the LNER had no leg to stand on. The victim, Mr Millar, was not much better. He was hospitalised for eight weeks, with multiple injuries and partial paralysis. Fortunately, he was able to limp away from court the following February £1,000 better off, with £100 costs. Mean-spiritedly, the LNER appealed against the legal costs, but with no apparent success.

The accident could only be the result of company management attempting to run a technically advanced, but labour-intensive, industry, with untrained volunteers. The previous accident, on the same afternoon as the St Margaret's tragedy, was the result of management running trains on a time-interval system – of the kind used on the earliest lines when locomotives ran at less than 30mph.

'Peaceful picketing', as it is termed, is really a farce...There can be no doubt at all that picketing prevented very considerable numbers of men from coming to work who otherwise would have done so...

So wrote one of the LNER district superintendents in reporting to his area general manager after the strike. Eight LNER employees in Scotland were dismissed after being convicted of offences involving violent picketing or intimidation. One such case involved an apprentice fitter assaulting two clerkesses in a city street, after they had left their office of the locomotive accountant at Cowlairs, on 6 May 1926. A £20 fine was followed by dismissal.

The LNER was quick to organise in-house catering and even sleeping accommodation at fourteen locations in Scotland, to reduce the need
for non-striking railway staff to cross picket-lines. Station restaurants were
opened specially for staff, while sleeping cars were marshalled for their use
in the centre roads at Edinburgh (Waverley) and Glasgow (Queen Street).
Other LNER sleeping accommodation varied from an engineer's van at
Anstruther to the bedrooms of the Palace Hotel at Aberdeen. On the other
side of the border, and as if to emphasise the difference in the respective
English and Scottish general strikes, in the railway centre of Carlisle, it
was found that the precautionary supply of sleeping accommodation was
unnecessary.

In the long-term, it may well be that such proof of forced withdrawal of
labour had an ameliorating effect on any managerial plans or desires for ret-
ribution against a workforce whose initial act of striking undoubtedly came
as a shock. The companies must have been glad to re-engage members of a
workforce who, quite literally, were irreplaceable.

The General Strike ended at noon on 12 May 1926. The strikers had won
no concessions from employers or government, and the miners fought on
alone. The rail companies counted their losses, amounting to an estimated
£6.94 million gross before the subtraction of unpaid wages.

Why was the confrontation between capital and labour so much more
trenchant in Scotland than in the south? There are two possible reasons:
in England, the seat of government was physically far removed from the
coalfields, creating an isolation zone which sheltered politicians and civil
servants from the colliers' wrath, preventing confrontations; secondly, in most
English cities, the leaders of those unions supporting the strike, particularly
railwaymen, reportedly spent much of their time on the telephone to union
headquarters in London. In Scotland, union HQ's and major branches were
located in Glasgow and Edinburgh – and the coal mines came right into the
suburbs of these cities.

In 1931 the International Union of Railways (IUR) published a history
of the previous decade in railway history, and had this to say of the General
Strike in Britain:

'[The rail companies] were forced to reduce their services owing to the
necessity for conserving what fuel they possessed, [so] much of their traffic
was thereby driven into the hands of their road competitors, in some cases
never to return'.

The study also made the point that road users did not have to husband fuel, since they were using imported fuel anyway – the UK was not self-sufficient in oil for another sixty years. (This ignores the fact that, in central Scotland at least, the principal road carrier, SMT, moved no buses from 4 to 11 May 1926.). The IUR seemed to be arguing that the railway suffered from being patriotic!

Once again, this English, or internationally derived, view of the strike, failed to take into account the reason for the sharp reduction of services in Scotland – what railway management called violence and intimidation.

In retrospect, there is no doubt that the trade unions concerned – and strictly speaking, the rail unions were involved in 'secondary' activity here, having no immediate grievance with their employers – went far beyond the bounds of what was acceptable in terms of peaceful picketing. While LNER officers were quick to argue, as shown at the opening of this chapter, that it was not just miners who showed a violent streak of militancy, and classed railwaymen with them, there seems little doubt that the worst cases of sabotage took place in coal-mining areas – Prestonpans, Newcraighall, Gorebridge and north Lanarkshire. The tampering with a vehicle brake at Ballater was very much an exception, although it does appear that aggressive picketing took place outside the gates of the engine shed and station yard.

The employers merely aggravated the problem by bringing in amateur labour. A more constructive reaction would have been to try to negotiate some kind of skeleton service of passenger and essential freight trains, to be operated with co-operation of the footplate and other two rail unions. Better still, if the railway companies had not made a point of opposing Geddes's plan for worker representation in the boardroom, the General Strike of 1926 might not have happened at all.

That the Scottish area of the LNER had been in the forefront of the (ill-advised) struggle to keep rail services going during the strike, is confirmed by a memo sent by chief general manager, Sir Ralph Wedgwood, to Calder on 20 May:

I don't think anyone had to face quite so complete a stoppage or so much mob-violence as you did in Scotland… [but] you had the situation well under control, and you were not, like some of our West Coast friends, in a fever of excitement.

4

Anglo-Scottish Express Trains I

If admirers of the LMS and LNER, whether English or Scottish, were asked to name the highlight of their companies' histories, they would probably nominate the halcyon days of the streamlined expresses from 1935 up to the outbreak of the Second World War. As far as Scottish-streamlined rail operations were concerned, the relevant period was in fact shorter, 1937–39, but the whole history of LMS and LNER operation across the Anglo-Scottish border is worthy of examination nevertheless.

Anglo-Scottish expresses were anything but streamlined in the days of steam before 1937, whether operated by the LMS, LNER or their constituent companies. In 1896, West and East Coast companies agreed on a protocol that no train starting its journey between London and Edinburgh or Glasgow, during daylight, would reach its destination in less than 495 minutes. With the exception of the occasional passage of accelerations – notably in 1901 – this was to be the rule for the next thirty-five years.

An accident at Preston was the spur for this arrangement, designed to reassure the public that the 'Races to the North', of 1888 and 1895, were not about to introduce a new 'devil-may-care' element into express passenger operation. The train involved in the Preston derailment was not in fact one of those racing against an East Coast rival, but this mattered not – public reassurance was deemed necessary.

This was all very well for the fevered atmosphere of the times, when cheap newspapers were beginning to exploit railway stories (usually to the disadvantage of the companies concerned), as any hints of express trains racing against a tightened schedule, or against those of another line, were deemed newsworthy. In July 1901, the Caledonian had been dragged into a short-lived contest because the *Daily Mail* insisted on publishing arrival times of West Coast London–Edinburgh trains – to the Caledonian's disadvantage – at a time when the North Eastern and North British were racing against each other. (See this author's *The Railway Race to Scotland 1901*.). But, long-term, the 1896 agreement threw a wet blanket over the embers of inter-company rivalry, snuffing out any accelerations before the Grouping took place.

After 1923, matters should have been very different. The new companies were, or should have been, anxious to attract public attention by highlighting their express services. Pacific locomotives now graced the locomotive studs of two former East-Coast companies (the GNR and NER), with good support from the Atlantics of no fewer than four companies (the above, plus GCR and NBR). On the West, the LNWR and Caledonian owned some fine 4-6-0s of considerable power, while the Midland had put its faith in a class of Compound 4-4-0s capable of working far beyond their designed capacity.

Things did not quite work out as might have been expected. While the LNER ordered no fewer than forty of Gresley's A1 Class (later A3), the LMS, incredibly, decided to perpetuate the Midland 4-4-0 design. It was a handsome tribute to the potential of these engines, although it must have been forgotten at Euston that their ability to steam at full-design capacity – and beyond – meant working the fireman to exhaustion. In any event, their tenders were unsuitable for long-distance travel, particularly in winter. Within three years, the LMS had to reverse its motive power policy, and order 4-6-0s virtually off the drawing-board, at North British Locomotive in Glasgow (which, ironically, had already delivered twenty of Gresley's A1s).

However, one operational matter that did not trouble the timetable planners of either East or West Coasts, was speed. The 1896 agreement was adhered to faithfully, even by the LMS and LNER, who inherited it. Indeed, if anything, this pernicious cartel was made worse.

Documents in the National Archives show that the LMS and LNER entered quite clinically into an agreement that, in a more media-active age, would have been quickly exposed as a cartel against the public interest. On 6 February 1924, the two companies arranged a high-level meeting at Liverpool Street to formalise inter-company contacts, which had been taking place over a number of weeks between middle-ranking staff. Passenger managers (Messrs Selway, Strang, and Lambert) were present from all three of the LNER's operational Areas. Curiously, the three LMS staff attending included the general superintendents from the Midland and Northern (i.e. Scottish) divisions, but not the Western (effectively the former LNWR main line). In the chair was William Clow, LNER Southern Area superintendent, although as a former Great Central man, he would hardly have much experience of Anglo-Scottish services.

The meeting agreed three points – that the two companies would recognise Glasgow as the LMS's principal destination in terms of Anglo-Scottish services, that Edinburgh and Aberdeen would be placed in the LNER's Area, and that:

> ... the whole of the Scotch [sic] Service should be agreed between the competing routes, and that the schedule of services should be signed [fixed] at least two months before each issue of the Time Tables. The schedules to be prepared each year alternatively by the L&NE and L&MS companies – the L&NE to prepare the schedule for 1924.

The word 'competing', in the first line of the above, is particularly ironic!

It was an extraordinary agreement. Any passenger dissatisfied with the timetabling of the LMS expresses over the border in 1924 should, by rights, have their complaint rerouted to the LNER! Nor was there any pussyfooting about the matter of time-fixing. No train, on either route, would travel between London and Edinburgh in less than eight hours, London and Glasgow in fifteen minutes more, and London–Aberdeen in eleven-and-a-half hours. Additionally, the LNER file contains a memo dated 19 February 1924, not intended for LMS eyes:

> ... it was noted that the L.M.S. had no intention at present of providing an early morning service to London and it was agreed therefore, that the question of arranging a service on the East Coast should not be proceeded with.

The complacency of the men who concluded this agreement was staggering. None of them could believe that anyone would dream of travelling between London and Glasgow, or Edinburgh, by bus. Was it any surprise that, within four years, they would be proved wrong? The decision not to provide an early morning departure – just because the 'rivals' had no plans for one – flew in the face of the fact that a huge majority of British people were up and about by 7 a.m. anyway.

Lord Monkswell, who believed that the railways were run just to suit their managements (see next chapter), would have given anything to have seen these meeting Minutes! We can nowadays; see the National Archives file references listed in the Bibliography.

Despite its intentionally slow schedule, the 'Flying Scotsman' was having new stock built for it in 1924 and 1928. The latter introduction included such novelties as a hairdressers and a cocktail bar, in addition to top-of-the-market restaurant facilities. Yet the timetable can only be described as dilatory, and it is a comment on the lack of professional standards in journalism that, even when the newspapers were tipped off about a 'speed control arrangement' in May 1928, they preferred to report on such trivialities as the number of haircuts and shaves administered to passengers on the first southbound non-stop 'Scotsman'. (Eighteen and three respectively, if the reader is interested!).

Running non-stop services over as long a distance as possible became a challenge for the East- and West-Coast companies, which could hardly do anything else to publicise their trains, other than emphasise their luxury status. The LNER had the advantage of the corridor tender, an eight-wheel vehicle, which, as well as carrying 9 tons of coal and 5,000 gallons of water, incorporated an 18in-wide passage to enable crews to be changed halfway through the journey. In the book *Non-Stop!*, this author stated his belief that Nigel Gresley did not patent the corridor tender idea in the UK, but research published by Gresley's biographer, Geoff Hughes, has revealed that the concept *was* in fact patented.

Although there were one-off challenges emanating from elsewhere – and an American Diesel claimed the crown for the longest journey ever (see this author's *Non Stop!*) – there was no rival for the LNER 'Flying Scotsman' service when it came to *daily* non-stop journeys over a distance of nearly 400 miles. Each day, the up and down 'Scotsmen' logged 786 miles between them, without an intermediate stop, during the summer months, from 1920 to 1939. They did so with a high degree of punctuality – although that is hardly to be wondered at, given the easy scheduling while the 1896 agreement held sway, which it did until 1932.

While the LNER set a tradition of non-stop running between King's Cross and Edinburgh – one which carried on, apart from the war years, until 1962 – the achievements of the LMS should not be ignored in this regard. Despite having no corridor tender available, the West-Coast company actually pre-empted the LNER as the latter prepared for its inauguration of the non-stop 'Flying Scotsman' in May 1928.

On the Friday before the LNER service was about to begin, the LMS secretly arranged to run the northbound 'Royal Scot' express in separate

Glasgow and Edinburgh sections. The first was headed by 'Royal Scot' 4-6-0 No.6113 *Cameronian*, which completed the 401-mile journey punctually. Driver David Gibson was at the controls, at least from Carlisle – the same man who had driven the only southbound train out of Central on the first day of the General Strike two years previously.

The Edinburgh run was perhaps more interesting in that the six-coach Edinburgh section was headed by nothing larger than a Midland Compound 4-4-0. This also accomplished the 400-mile journey punctually, with driver Ballantine of Edinburgh's Dalry Road 'conducting' the English crew when north of Carlisle. Both locomotives had tenders with coal rails heightened to accommodate more fuel. The tenders would also have to serve as toilets, since the LMS had made no arrangements whatsoever for the crews to answer calls of nature.

The company was completely reliant on the crews' co-operation to establish these runs, both longer than King's Cross–Waverley, and both a British, indeed European, record for non-stop running that stood for twenty years. (The LMS should have thought seriously about paying patent fees to allow it to use Gresley's patented tender; the LMS main line was longer than the LNER's, and they could have claimed a world record for daily non-stop running.).

Incidentally, as well as being one of the few men at Polmadie to cross the picket-line in 1926 – which must have taken some courage – driver Gibson was a traffic manager's dream. In 1929 he was at the controls of No.6127 *Novelty*, when it ran a special train 395 miles from Glenboig, north-east of Glasgow, non-stop all the way to Euston. Gibson and his fireman worked for over eight hours without a break, and without toilet facilities. The LMS directors and management should have been ashamed of themselves.

In passing, one curious operational policy on the LNER should be mentioned. Gresley's remit in constructing larger, and ever more powerful, passenger locomotives for the East-Coast lines, was in response to the challenge of hauling express trains, which regularly loaded up to fifteen or sixteen bogies. With their steel frames and teak bodies, a train made up of LNER express coaches would weigh in at some 450 to 500 tons, and that's without including passengers and luggage. What is curious, looking back, is that these heavy train rakes – or 'consists' as American railroaders called them – were a matter of policy. In other words, even if the traffic did not warrant it, an express would be made up to a tare weight of 400 tons or more, irrespective of passenger demand for that particular service. This came under particular review in the summer of 1933.

In that year, a young LNER traffic apprentice named L.W. Ibbotson was unusually given a travelling remit to journey up and down the East-Coast main line sampling his company's product – the express trains themselves, their seating accommodation, their catering and sleeping facilities, the conduct of their crews. His finished report can be found in the National Archives, and sometimes makes amusing reading, as we witness Mr Ibbotson running his finger over un-dusted surfaces in his sleeping carriage, testing the toilets for their flushing efficiency, and harassing the restaurant car stewards to bring him ice cream, even when it was not on the menu!

One point which he made, and which soon provoked a reaction from his superiors in the traffic department, was about the surplus seating available on some of the trains he sampled. On the 5.10 p.m. to Leeds out of Edinburgh (in post-war years the 'North Briton'), Mr Ibbotson found thirty-one third-class passengers scattered throughout four coaches, while the Sunday 11.30 a.m. King's Cross–Waverley, 'could have done with at least four third [-class coaches] fewer than was actually employed'. His report went straight to Sir Ralph Wedgwood, with the members of the Joint Superintendents' and Passenger Managers' Committee scrambling to add their responses. One point the managers were at pains to make was that a rake of coaching stock might be only lightly occupied in one direction, but packed full on the opposite leg of the diagram.

No consideration appears to have been given to alternative approaches to this problem of variable public usage of timetabled trains. For example, shorter coaching rakes could have been reinforced from pools of coaching stock kept available at major passenger stations. Nor does there appear to have been much notice taken of a *cri de coeur* from a company fireman who wrote to the *LNER Magazine*, deploring the policy of 'trailing enormous trains of 30-ton to 34-ton bogies [carriages] about, with a few passengers in each', with employees like himself having, 'to heave coal into these monster [locomotives]'. One again we see staff welfare rating zero on a scale of none to ten. The LMS was not the only company which treated its footplate staff like serfs.

It should not be imagined that no reconstruction at all had been carried out on the East- and West-Coast routes themselves. On the contrary, both LNER and LMS were busy improving their main trunk-routes north of the border.

On the East Coast, the border area itself presented a potential problem. Berwick-on-Tweed Station constituted the southern destination of the North British, and they had spared every expense in building it! According

to O.S. Nock, 'it was built in masonry largely recovered from the demolition of the medieval castle [which the company had cheerfully carried out
with only two protests from local residents]... but the foundations were
unsound'. Mr Nock believed that the station nearly collapsed within a year
of construction, but whether this is exaggerated or not, the fact is that a
5mph speed restriction was necessary through what *The Times* called the
'squalid platforms' (no more than 12ft wide). The North British began to
improve matters with the installation of a loop on the up side during the
First World War, and a new overbridge was opened in 1921, but the LNER
resolved to finish the job early in 1924.

It was decided to replace the existing structure with an 800ft-island
platform connected by footbridge and electrically powered parcels
hoists to the approach road on the up side. An estimate of £42,970 was
agreed by the Works Committee, and tenders invited. The company was
delighted to accept a tender from Hugh Symington & Sons of Glasgow for
£38,297 13/4*d*, (£38,297 67p) although experience should have told
the LNER officials that contractors who underestimate costs often have
problems carrying out the actual work (the Killin branch worked by the
Caledonian was a famous example). Symingtons were bankrupt within
eighteen months, although, curiously, the committee papers for October
1925 show that the LNER was satisfied with the progress of the reconstruction at Berwick, which was presumably being finished by contractors
appointed by the firm of liquidators. The latter asked to be excused the
contractual obligation to be responsible for all maintenance for twelve
months after completion – for which their fee was 'docked' by £100 – but
it appears that the LNER emerged unscathed from what could have been
a major early setback in its programme to improve the East-Coast main
line.

While this new realignment required a slowing for through trains, particularly in the up direction, the proximity of the Royal Border Bridge
necessitated a slowing anyway. But it was an improvement on 5mph!

Also swept away by the new administration was the NBR locomotive
depot immediately north-west of the station, and configured as a semi-
roundhouse. It boasted thirteen roads, the central one covered by an archway
supporting the depot water tank and a clock. Plans had been drawn up by
the company to replace this, but it was not until 1924 that the new LNER
demolished the structure, sensibly sending NBR engines, operating the
East-Coast line and the Duns and Eyemouth branches, to the former NER
shed at Tweedmouth. This was to have unexpected consequences in later

years, when the Tweedmouth shedmaster found that services on Scottish branch-lines did not observe the same Bank Holidays as their English counterparts, requiring him to provide for trains advertised in two quite different timetables.

Berwick was not the only station on the route requiring reconstruction, with the LNER taking Dunbar in hand not long afterwards. Through lines bypassing the station were built just to the south of it, although a 60mph-restriction was necessary here. Nevertheless, this was an improvement; modernisation at Berwick and Dunbar should have been worth more than five minutes in time-saving to an express not stopping at these stations. In fact, this acceleration failed to materialise – the dead hand of the 1890s still held sway.

In 1945, the LNER prepared plans to install water-troughs between Drem and Ballencreiff, some 18 miles from Edinburgh, at an estimated cost of £11,200. Despite being granted 'first priority' status (in comparison, the fitting of colour-light signalling from Edinburgh to Berwick was 'second priority'), the troughs were never laid.

On the west, the LMS was quicker, and more effective, in addressing the problem of water provision. The Caledonian had not installed any water-troughs north of Carlisle, relying instead on double-bogie tenders to carry an appropriate supply for its 4-6-0s and its illustrious 'Dunalastairs'. It was probably not worth the LMS perpetuating this type of tender – there were already nine sets of troughs on the WCML south of Carlisle (compared to six on the entire East Coast) – and anyway, an eight-wheel vehicle would have dwarfed the Midland 4-4-0, the new choice of express motive power!

Troughs were installed by the LMS at Mossband, immediately south of Gretna Junction, where the former GSW main line went off westwards (and still does, although singled for some reason from Gretna to Annan). A second set was laid out 2 miles south of Strawfrank Junction, Carstairs. Although the latter set could be used by services to and from Glasgow and Edinburgh, they were intended more to benefit trains going to and from Perth. During the 1895 race to Aberdeen, the 150 miles from Carlisle to Perth was one of the most difficult stretches to be run non-stop and at high speed, with Beattock summit thrown in as an additional test of locomotive and crew.

On the former G&SWR, a set of troughs was laid at around the same time between New Cumnock and Kirkconnel, presumably to permit non-stop running on Euston–Glasgow night trains diverted away from the

West–Coast main line. With these two installations in Scotland, and one immediately south of the border, the LMS had provided its crews with the option of replenishing locomotives' water supply at speed.

5

Investment and Economy

By the end of the 1920s, the LNER experienced a drop in passenger journeys of 20 per cent, while in Scotland, rail managers reported a fall in goods traffic, particularly from the pithead. Buses and lorries were becoming a common sight on Britain's roads, even if the private car was still something of a rarity.

It was becoming clear to the management of the 'Big Two' that economies would have to be made. Consequently, the colourful liveries so proudly exhibited, discussed, and selected in 1923, were replaced by lined black for all but express passenger locomotives from around 1928. Since LNER Scottish Area experienced a 10 per cent drop in the number of engine cleaners available in that year, the liveries – certainly of goods engines – were rapidly becoming invisible anyway under the grime.

Railway managements may have realised that history was repeating itself, with the train filling the role previously occupied by the stagecoach and the canal barge. Although Geoff Hughes has remarked that, 'no one was thinking of closing railways in 1923', this may have been true in the UK as a whole; in fact, closures began in Scotland from the start of the new company's existence.

On the LNER, there was a prompt move to withdraw the branch service to Macmerry in East Lothian. This seems to have been fairly uncontroversial; it was, in effect, a branch from another branch, the line to Gifford, and Macmerry residents could access stations to the north of them on the East-Coast main line. But the closure of the Granton branch in 1925 was a different matter, and the ructions it caused are uniquely preserved in a file in the National Archives.

The Granton branch was historic in that it had provided the ferry point for trains to Burntisland, and then Dundee and Aberdeen, running originally through the Scotland Street tunnel from Edinburgh's Canal Street Station, opened in 1847. In 1862, the North British took over the much-renamed company, latterly known as the Edinburgh & Northern, and from 1868, trains reached Granton from Waverley via Abbeyhill. (Poignantly, this was the route used by the service which went down with the first Tay Bridge in 1879.). There was also a fairly bustling service between Granton and Scotland Street, even after the closure of Canal Street, at the top end of the tunnel running up from Scotland Street.

Historic or not, the LNER was quite unimpressed by the traffic figures generated by the branch. With rail ferry traffic lost after 1890, when the Forth Bridge opened, only £2,000 revenue was received from the line in 1924, despite some 65,000 passenger journeys being made on it. Running costs came to nearly £5,000 in that year. (While the ferry continued, it handled road traffic, the revenue being entered in a different account.).

The files show that, in the following year, James Calder was surprisingly quick to give his blessing to closure, and after the chairman had approved, all department heads were circulated, and gave their approval. Even Messrs Slaughter, the company leasing advertising boards on Granton Station, with its unusually low platform, was informed. The only people who did not know about the impending closure were the passengers!

Closure was advertised as late as 21 October 1925, for the following 2 November, and with two Sundays intervening, this was effectively ten days' notice of closure. Needless to say, the Transport Users' Consultative Committee was still some twenty-five years in the future.

But the LNER was going to have to learn to close branch-lines properly! Local councillors soon headed a delegation to the LNER offices at Waterloo Place, arguing that Newhaven fishwives – traditionally very much part of the Edinburgh scene, going from house to house with baskets of fish on their backs – would suffer inconvenience by the closure of the intermediate station at Trinity. However, the company was able to prove that most of these redoubtable ladies used Bonnington Road station on the North Leith branch, and the point was also made that the Granton ferry was busiest on Sundays, when the branch did not operate.

The LNER managers no doubt patted themselves on the back for dealing with this opposition, and closure went ahead as scheduled. But their complacency was premature. Three weeks after closure, a local lawyer complained about this transport loss to his MP, Capt. Wedgwood Benn (father to the present Tony Benn). This resulted in the Ministry of Transport asking for a written justification for closure, and the LNER was back at square one.

James Calder ordered Messrs Strang (passenger manager) and Stemp (area superintendent) to draw up a document for the Ministry, which they undertook with some alacrity. Unfortunately, the company solicitor chimed in with an independent letter to the Ministry, insisting that there had been no complaints about closure, which was hardly the case considering the deputation that had to be dealt with. Fortunately for the company, the lawyer taking the complaint to Benn had made a speculative, and quite inaccurate, statement about the branch's costs and revenue, and this did his case no good at all. Nevertheless, the Ministry had to wait until 30 January 1926 to receive a detailed statement on this closure, and the records indicate that a considerable number of highly placed officials – including, of course, the principal LNER officer in Scotland – were engaged in making this presentation to their political overseers. At one stage, they were claiming that they had the legal right to close any line they liked – probably a true statement, but one hardly likely to improve relations with the public! It could and should have been all so different.

It would be pleasant to report that the experience of closing Granton proved so administratively awkward for the LNER, that they resolved never to close another branch ever again. Of course, we know that this was not quite the case!

The first three years of the 1930s saw a flurry of closures on both the LMS and LNER; indeed, the number of service withdrawals at this time was to be unequalled for a further twenty years. What almost certainly triggered the closures following that of the Granton branch had something to do with the two rail companies investing in quite a different form of transport – the bus.

Since being established by William Thomson with capital of £50,000 in 1905, Scottish Motor Traction (SMT) had become one of the fastest growing bus companies in the country. Based in Edinburgh, the company soon discovered that the poor location of the Waverley Station detracted from the effectiveness of the entire suburban rail network. It was widely believed that the royal family always preferred arriving at the LMS's Princes Street Station for their annual visit, so a commuter having to travel *daily* into central Edinburgh was unlikely to be any more enamoured with the Waverley, which is far below street level. Escalators were first called for by the local press as early as 1925, but even today their installation seems as far away as ever. Additionally, Edinburgh's municipal trams were cable-operated until 1921, providing music-hall comedians with endless material. No wonder SMT was able to expand its services so quickly.

Company records show that both the LMS and LNER were prepared to face their tormentors and deal directly with the road lobby on the grounds of: 'if you can't beat them…'. Legislation passed in 1928 – the Railway Road Powers Act – allowed the 'Big Four' to invest in road services where it appeared appropriate to do so. As well as talking to SMT, it appears that the LMS and LNER began dialogues with such road firms as Pickfords, Tillings, and British Automobile.

But it is the Scottish bus company which concerns us, and in 1928 SMT's capital stood at £400,000. After preliminary discussions, both rail companies' representatives were confident that they could conclude an agreement for the LMS and LNER to each take a substantial £100,000 shareholding in a newly constituted SMT company by 1 November of that year.

Things did not quite work out that way.

Despite SMT's managing director (referred to in the documents as 'Bailie Thomson') enjoying a £10,000 retainer in shares, and the promise of a £5,000 annual salary to head the new company, negotiations seemed somewhat tardy, stretching well into the following year. Meanwhile, in February 1929, SMT took a controlling interest in Alexander's of Falkirk and Midland Bus of Airdrie. Two months later, SMT was offering an Edinburgh–Carlisle service, rivalling both the rail companies, and extending to Keswick for the summer months.

Not surprisingly, by the time the old SMT was being formally wound up and the new company registered in the summer of 1929, the bus group's capital had shot up to £1.5 million, inevitably downsizing the rail companies' investment. This would not have mattered so much had the LMS and LNER secured their position in the new boardroom. In fact, they received only two directorships out of a total of ten, although they would have the right of veto over appointments to three other places.

Suffice to say that the rail companies' investment in an expanding bus business was poorly handled. Possibly, this was because of the need for LMS and LNER staff to liaise, not just with SMT officials, but among their own four offices in London and Scotland. When the LNER produced its £100,000-cheque in August 1929, it came from London on the personal authority of the chief general manager, Sir Ralph Wedgwood. Meanwhile, the LMS file contains memos between senior company officials asking for background details on one of their LNER opposite numbers.

Dealing with a family concern which knew the road business thoroughly, had meant that rail officials, who were unfamiliar with the business and even with each other, were always going to be at a disadvantage in negotiating with one of Scotland's leading entrepreneurs. William Johnston Thomson was a phenomenon, having left school at twelve, trained as an engineer from an apprenticeship, employed his wife in the office while getting his own company under way (not exactly common practice in Edwardian times), and owned 3,000 vehicles by 1947. He was knighted by George V at Holyroodhouse in 1934, by which time he was Lord Provost of Edinburgh, having been elected to the Haymarket ward thirteen years previously. No wonder mere railway administrators found themselves outclassed by him!

If this opinion seems to be the result of retrospective analysis, note that the archival records include a letter from the LMS solicitor, James Wilson, to Sir Arthur Rose (a member of the LMS Local Committee and a District Commissioner during the General Strike), in May 1929: 'I cannot say that I would approve the manner in which the negotiations have been gone about, but that is now-a-days not a matter for the solicitor'.

The railways' purchase of what was meant to be a substantial interest in road transport was something of a botch-up. Although the highly respected historian of Scottish Motor Traction, the late David Hunter, recorded that the LMS and LNER had purchased 'a half-share between them' in the bus company, this would seem to refer to the negotiations as conducted, inconclusively, in 1928 (and it would surely have been a one-third share between them, i.e. £200,000 out of a proposed new capitation of £600,000). It could, however, be argued that, in theory, the railways had a say in the filling of five out of ten directors' chairs. Within twenty years, the LMS and LNER were each drawing dividends from SMT to the tune of £228,631 (in 1946) – not bad for an initial investment of £100,000 each! But one suspects that the rail companies had hardly invested in SMT to see a rival go from strength to strength.

Far from placing a firm hand on the tiller of SMT, the LMS and LNER found that they had considerably less influence, never mind control, in a company whose fortunes were strengthened by the railways' support, but where the direction of the company effectively remained with the existing directors of this family based concern. Instead, the loss of passenger services on such branch-lines as Annan (Shawhill), Bankfoot, Dolphinton and Fochabers (LMS), and Boddam, Gullane, Dalmeny–Ratho and Lauder (LNER) followed within four years of the ink drying on the agreement with SMT. In the case of Dolphinton, a village honoured by branches owned by *both* of the rail companies, there was an attempt by SMT to cover for the closure of the LMS branch by rerouting its Edinburgh–Lanark service via Dolphinton and Carstairs village, but substitution of bus for train was surely not the only motivation for rail investing in road.

As Mr Hunter observes dryly in his company history, 'this major financial development did not produce any evident change in the company's
[SMT's] operations'.

Despite the less-than-impressive handling of their negotiations with SMT,
the railways' investing in the encroaching bus services showed a certain real-
ism – although the railway enthusiast might wonder if a more selective
response from LMS and LNER managers to the petrol-engined rival could
have been adopted if the rail companies had more power in the boardroom.
Using buses as 'feeders' to branch-line termini, for example, restructuring
rail fares and timetables, replacing many station staff with on-board conduc-
tor-guards, all could have been introduced if the infiltration of SMT by the
rail companies had been more successful.

The staffing of country stations in particular was an area where economies could have been made – and without having to relegate stations to
un-staffed halts. As late as the 1930s, the junction station of St Boswells,
halfway down the LNER's Waverley Route, required enough staff to see off
simultaneous departures from the north and south bay platforms, on no less
than three occasions daily! The slightest staggering of departure times could
have affected an obvious economy here. If redundancies resulted, at least
there would be other employment opportunities on a system which might
not have been required to retract so severely if a more positive policy had
been pursued towards less remunerative lines.

Not all branch-lines lost passenger services at this time. Both companies
experimented with steam-powered railcars, but the LMS appears to have
had less faith in these, and there was no nationwide re-equipping on the
company's Scottish branch-lines. Some cascading of pre-Grouping stock
took place, and the Moffat branch was one where former LNWR and
Lancashire & Yorkshire vehicles took up employment at various times, until
Nationalisation. The working timetables instructed staff that these 'steam
motor carriages' had a 'self-contained non-detachable engine'.

In later years, some LNWR push-pull units powered by 1P 2-4-2 tanks
were based at Dumfries and Beattock, being described in the timetables as
'motor trains' but, on the Moffat and Biggar lines, propelling of a passenger
vehicle was permitted anyway, even with the driver at the rear of the train!
Working instructions ordered the guard to keep 'a sharp look-out'! On such
branches as Killin, Ballachullish, to say nothing of Leith and the Cathcart
Circle, the former 'Caley' 0-4-4 tank was the usual motive power – on conventionally operated services – in some cases almost right up to closure.
Suffice to say that there was little evidence of any major LMS investment in

its branch-line network north of the border, except, of course, in the rival bus system.

In contrast, the LNER did at least provide new stock for many Scottish branch-lines, and some suburban services. When attending the 1924 Empire Exhibition at Wembley, where his 'Flying Scotsman' rivalled a GWR 'Castle' for pride of place, Nigel Gresley took a great interest in a steam railcar exhibited by the Sentinel Co. of Shrewsbury. As a result, the LNER placed an order for eighty of these, delivered over a seven-year period from 1925. Of these, fifteen found their way north of the border, where they were to be found from Silloth (admittedly *south* of the border, but an ex-NBR line), to Aberdeenshire.

To modern eyes, there is something grotesque in seeing a square-ended passenger coach complete with a chimney at one end, and it is no great surprise that they were referred to as 'chip vans' by some unkind members of the public. They were difficult to operate and were sluggish hill-climbers, losing speed if given a coach, or even a van, to haul. Commenting on their work in Scotland, Maj. Stemp reported that they were more susceptible to breakdowns than more conventional forms of traction. Their being named after traditional stage-coaches was an interesting idea, although the choice of a green-and-white livery was an example of poor public relations. This prompted many passengers to assume that the SMT company was taking over rail operations – for this was a colour-scheme seen daily by that company's road passengers – when in fact the railways were investing heavily, or at least, *thought* they were investing heavily, in bus operation.

An archival report on the use of Sentinels on the former NBR Carlisle–Silloth service indicates impressively increased revenue – 31 per cent in July 1928, and no less than 127 per cent in the following month. But, as BR Scottish Region was to discover when introducing Diesel railbuses in the late 1950s, single-coach trains could initially stimulate patronage which their limited capacity prevented them from satisfying. Indeed, BR would use this argument to justify closing branch-lines without ever having experimented with Diesel railcars or buses on a particular branch, arguing that this new form of traction would be likely to over-stimulate public patronage. (The sheer negativity of this argument made it difficult for closure protestors to combat, as L.T.C. Rolt pointed out in his autobiographical volume, *Landscape with Figures*.). Some of these Sentinels lasted to immediate post-war days, but did nothing in the long-term to arrest the decline in branch-line use.

Another form of transport which enjoyed railway company investment was the aeroplane. The legislation establishing the grouped rail companies allowed them powers to operate air services as far as 20 degrees east. A glance at an atlas will open up the extraordinary aspect of LMS or LNER Airways, or whatever, flying in and out of Poland, Yugoslavia, North Africa, Sweden and so on! While the new companies were too busy simply 'getting on with running the railway', there was a move to invest in air services in the early 1930s, with the initiative coming from, not too surprisingly, Sir Eric Geddes, the architect of the 1923 Amalgamation in the first place, and by then chairman of Imperial Airways. All this will be dealt with in the chapter 'Off the Rails'.

The historian cannot help remarking on what little investment both the LMS and LNER put into their freight services. Additions or improvements to goods depots and shunting yards in Scotland were fragmentary and scattered; no great marshalling yards were created. Writing in 1958, G. Freeman Allen, editor of the magazine *Trains Illustrated*, quoted a senior rail manager as complaining that Scotland's eighty or so shunting yards were, 'chiefly a heritage, not from the LMS and LNER, but from much farther back, from the pre-1923 companies'. It was left to BR to modernise in the 1950s – much too late, and failing to take into account such innovations as containerisation and dedicated single-owner train formations, which required no marshalling.

The resulting abominations on the landscape at Millerhill (Edinburgh), Perth, and Kingmoor (Carlisle) caused offence to local residents and passing travellers alike, in their destruction of good agricultural land. The author recalls travelling in the early 1960s on a Waverley Route express, which crawled past the huge area being cleared to make way for Millerhill yard. An elderly-lady passenger surveyed the blighted landscape, and announced, 'the whole thing's a waste of money'. As a precocious schoolboy who maintained what I fancied was a knowledgeable monitoring of rail operations, I wondered what on earth she knew about it. But of course she was right! Gerard Fiennes wrote in his memoirs that Millerhill was a 'white elephant'. Perhaps a little more investment in Scottish freight facilities by the LMS and LNER, at a time long before motorways were created, might have been more timely.

However, it would be wrong to suggest that railway companies between the wars were unaware of the importance of offering fitted freight services to their industrial customers. ('Fitted', incidentally, meant that wagons were equipped with brakes which could be operated from the locomotive, as in passenger trains. It seems incredible nowadays but probably 90 per cent of railway wagons in the age of steam could only be braked by hand, by a shunter running alongside a moving train. This was in addition to a hand-brake in the guard's van, but an ill-timed application of this could break a train in two.).

In the summer of 1928, the LNER introduced a fast-fitted freight intended to run overnight from Glasgow (High Street) – London Marylebone. After incorporating traffic from Perth and Leith Walk, the service departed Niddrie West at 6.10 p.m., arriving at Marylebone at 7.07 a.m. the next day. Average loading in the summer months was thirty-six vehicles, increasing to forty-seven as the winter drew in. It was, or should have been, a portent of what was to come in the field of overland freight transport, and a wider application of fitted-freight vehicles would surely have been appropriate.

Unfortunately, when a Royal Commission on Transport reported only three years later, it was highly critical of the railways' freight-carrying performance, pointing out that the average container – and there were precious few of them on Britain's freight trains – contained only 4 tons of cargo. Needless to say, when BR introduced the overnight 'Condor' service between Glasgow and London in 1956, no less than twenty-five years later, the same capacity container was still in use.

'Fast-fitted' trains were not enough to wean railway managers away from the concept which they had known all of their careers – that of a lucrative freight load consisting of hundreds of tons of coal or other minerals, being trundled along at 5mph, headed by a locomotive built perhaps fifty years earlier and undoubtedly accounts-expired, with a guard in a van, all of the vehicles having been built by the previous owners.

So, mineral traffic in particular carried on under the 'Big Two', much as it had under the pre-Grouping companies – the NBR and Caledonian had probably created an infrastructure for handling coal traffic that required little or no improvement until demand for the product changed, particularly with the slowing in export markets in the 1960s. The ambitious 'reconstruction' plans drawn up by the LNER and circulated internally from July 1945 (see chapter 'Towards Nationalisation'), provide ample proof that freight was one area which the company had hitherto failed to invest in, simply carrying on with the facilities put in place by the North British.

Proposing new yards for Alloa and Portobello, together with a new water supply at Cadder (where locomotive requirements ran at more than twice the guaranteed supply) are only three examples of a company belatedly trying to compensate for a previous lack of investment – and by 1945, of course, it was too late.

Investing in stations was an obvious area where the 'Big Two' rail companies could have made a direct public statement about their commitment to
future rail services. In fact, the early example of Berwick-on-Tweed Station
was not to become the first of many re-buildings; indeed, the LNER may
have found that project, essential though it was, to be a somewhat scarring
experience, as we have seen.

The LNER's two biggest stations in Scotland were Edinburgh (Waverley)
and Glasgow (Queen Street) – in fact, the former was the biggest LNER
station in the UK. Neither received any major investment – as far as passenger facilities were concerned – in LNER days, apart from public-address
systems from the 1930s onwards. Conspicuously, despite the dire need for
escalators at Waverley, none were added, and, as the local newspaper predicted, the suburban rail system would die as a result. The signalling *was*
improved, as will be related later. The company's two stations in Dundee
remained largely as built (counting the east terminus, although effectively
a joint station), and the eye searches the Scottish landscape in vain for any
major station reconstruction. (Perth and Aberdeen were not wholly LNER
stations, but were not great centres of investment by the LMS either.).

The 1945 reconstruction plans drawn up by the LNER dwelled mainly
on the need to improve goods and motive-power depots, with most of the
station rebuilding being of a minor nature. However, Partick, Singer, and
Dalmuir were to be given priority for renovation work, 'following air raid
damage'.

The LMS regarded Glasgow (Central) as the centrepiece of its Scottish
passenger operations, and with good reason. Enlarged as recently as 1906,
it was the jewel in the Caledonian crown and had already seen considerable investment, not least in its power signalling and points, controlled by a
374-lever frame. The LMS made some improvements to this around 1930,
including the installation of track-circuiting.

Buchanan Street was a different matter and, with its Edinburgh and
English traffic lost to Central some decades earlier, some necessary rebuilding
took place in the 1930s. The platform awnings there always had a temporary air, until the LMS replaced them with steel-framed glazed awnings (but
only 'second hand', from Ardrossan North!). This was in 1932, when a new
concourse façade, consisting of a steel frame covered with wood cladding,
was built.

In their history of Glasgow stations, Johnston and Hume opine, 'in
this form, the station had something of the charm of a country terminus', although they also quote the late Prof. Jack Simmons as describing

Buchanan Street Station as, 'easily the most abominable in Western Europe'. It is abominable no more, having closed in 1966, when most of its services were transferred to Queen Street.

Glasgow (St Enoch) was another pre-Grouping terminus which had to soldier on with what it already had, but as the headquarters of the former G&SWR, it had been well served by that railway. It boasted Britain's biggest signalbox, one of 488 levers, with power-signalling, but with the points operated manually. Apart from the installation of colour-light signalling by the LMS by 1933 (with a certain Mr Nock involved), this terminus operated cheerfully and efficiently until the end of its working life in much the same manner as when the G&SWR handed it over at the end of 1922. If it was in decline, the downward path was a slow one; in the last full year of the LMS's existence, 1947, St Enoch handled 1.26 million outgoing passenger journeys, and this had fallen only to 1.23 million in its final full year of operation, 1965. This was exclusive of season-ticket sales and parcels revenue. The value of St Enoch to the public transport network was undeniable.

Nor did Edinburgh's Princes Street Station fare better than any other terminus. Its main improvement came in 1937 with the provision of new signalling but, curiously, semaphores were utilised, at a time when Waverley was receiving its colour-lights.

Interestingly, the finest station rebuilding in the first half of the twentieth century can be found at a comparatively remote outpost of the former 'South West' – at Girvan in south Ayrshire. At this, the last major centre before southbound trains head for the wilds of Wigtownshire, the station buildings on the northbound platform here are an eye-catching example of mid-twentieth-century architecture. Before crediting the LMS, however – it was in January 1946 that a major fire made reconstruction necessary – it should be recalled that this building, so quintessentially 1930s, in fact opened in April 1951.

At the time of writing, the plans for these buildings have not been unearthed in the National Archives, and it is unclear to what extent the LMS was responsible for drawing-up such an arresting design. Given that company's record for cost-saving, it seems more likely that the nationalised industry was left to carry out the necessary reconstruction; more information on this rebuilding would be welcome. The 'new' buildings have been refurbished with the help of a Scottish Executive grant, although the attractive metalwork railings could, at the time of writing, benefit from some additional maintenance.

Curiously, both LMS and LNER constructed un-staffed halts at various locations where there was obvious population growth, but this occurred even when existing stations appeared to be over-staffed. In Edinburgh, for example, the LNER opened a halt at Balgreen on the Corstorphine branch, while the LMS created un-staffed stopping places at East Pilton and House o'Hill on the Leith and Barnton branches, respectively. Hailes platform, on the Colinton–Balerno loop, was established to serve golfers. Casual use by sportsmen was a perfectly valid reason for providing an un-staffed stopping-place, but whether this was the best way to provide for the needs of areas of increasing population, as on the Barnton branch, its surely debateable.

While none of the Scottish urban stations underwent any major rebuilding, Edinburgh's Waverley was at least re-signalled in an extensive engineering development which took no less than three years to complete. In the days of semaphore signals, the prospect off the platform ends at each end of the station – which has of course a through configuration as well as terminal bays and dock platforms – was obscured by huge gantries of signals. These were controlled by two major boxes in the middle of the running lines, while there were necessary subsidiary boxes below street level halfway along the through platform lengths, as well as a box in Princes Street Gardens, and larger boxes at Haymarket to the west and Abbeyhill on the east.

The western side of the station was converted first, with 205 miniature levers in the power box controlling not just signals and points, but also platform indicators displaying information to the drivers of arriving trains. Two of the five boxes replaced in this stage of rebuilding were converted into studios for station announcements. This stage was completed on 4 October 1936, when the *Scotsman* newspaper commented that, 'the old semaphore signal arms are now lying in piles at the side of the tracks'.

But it was to be no less than another twenty-five months before the east end of the station was converted. Here, the existing central cabin boasted what was, at one time, the record number of semaphore levers (260) in a single frame. The new system replaced this with a new power box (like the West box) on the down side of the tracks, which now had colour-light signalling from Haymarket Central on the west, all the way eastwards to Abbeyhill Junction. A current of 110 volts was run through the rails to provide track-circuiting in 195 individual sections, using the city's power supply, but with a 38hp-petrol generator available for emergency use. It was a wise fallback – it was not so long previously that the Corporation power-station staff had to ask a local butcher not to switch on his mincing machine at peak periods as it used too much of the city supply!

The Waverley Route was conspicuous in its low investment share from the LNER, the 1945 'Reconstruction' document (see chapter 'Towards Nationalisation') focusing on the need for modernising loco facilities at Hawick. Galashiels had benefited, in 1935, from virtually the only investment on this route from the LNER, with its signalling being centralised in a new box at the north end of the down platform, taking over the functions of the two junction boxes for the Peebles and Selkirk lines outside the station area.

Robert Collier, the third Baron Monkswell, had an interesting theory about the lack of investment in the railways for over fifty years from the end of the nineteenth century. He believed that, around the middle of that century:

> It very soon occurred to the [railway managers] that all they had to do to secure for themselves a quiet untroubled existence was to agree with one another not to compete, and, as nearly as possible, to do nothing in the way of introducing better services or technical improvements.

When the historian looks back at the incredibly slow introduction of such innovations as track-circuiting, cab-signalling, aluminium rolling-stock, roller-bearings, continuous freight braking, diesel and electric power, to say nothing of such improvements in steam-power design as double chimneys, mechanical stoking, and new ejector arrangements, it is difficult to argue with Monkswell.

In particular, the February 1924 pact between LMS and LNER to prevent accelerations on Anglo-Scottish services, as shown in the last chapter, was drawn up at managerial level only, with no directors present. Yet it is surely unarguable that policy decisions such as this – and agreeing with a rival company not to compete with them is undoubtedly policy of a kind – should be decided in the boardroom.

To take only one example of calculated lack of investment – the terrible accident at Quintinshill in 1915, when 227 men died – could probably have been averted if track-circuiting had been fitted. True, this was not the opinion of the Ministry of Transport reporter who conducted the subsequent inquiry, although his justification for the non-installation of this simple and inexpensive system, scarcely stands up to examination. He opined that the view from the signalbox was good in both directions, when in fact this was not equally true for locomotive crews whose sightlines were obscured by a bend to the north (as O.S. Nock discovered on a footplate trip); in any event, the loss of visibility at night or in mist surely invalidated the reporter's comment. As early as 1880, a Ministry inspector reporting on the Nine Elms accident had suggested that track-circuiting would have prevented it happening. Indeed, the Ministry of Transport official examining an accident uncannily similar, although mercifully less catastrophic, than Quintinshill, later in 1915 in County Durham, recommended the installation of track-circuiting. Many years later, in 1952, a chief inspector of railways remarked that one formal accident inquiry in every ten would have been rendered unnecessary if track-circuiting had been in widespread operation – one suspects this is a conservative estimate.

Track-circuiting had been perfected as early as 1872, but this cheap and effective means of train control and accident prevention was not exactly introduced quickly on to Britain's – never mind Scotland's – railways. The Caledonian failed to install it at Quintinshill (near Gretna), or anywhere else. The LMS and LNER were not much better, applying it piecemeal, and mainly at major termini where speeds were low anyway. It was, however, present in 1937 at Castlecary, the site of the worst Scottish accident since Quintinshill, but was not locked into the signalling system, and was ignored by a distressed signalman when giving a correct reading. (Accidents occurring in Scotland during LMS and LNER days are dealt with in a later chapter.).

Public safety was very important, but so were shareholder dividends.

Cab-signalling was not commonplace on Britain's railways until the 1950s, but should certainly have been considered for earlier application. Around 1895, the North Eastern Railway had equipped two stretches of the East-Coast main line, south of Berwick, with a mechanical invention of Sir Vincent Raven's, where a trigger between the rails would catch a special fitting under the locomotive, and indicate to the crew whether the 'distant' signal was in their favour or not. The scheme began to prove troublesome with age, but was surely worth modernising. In fact, the LNER *dismantled* it in 1933 – two years before the 'Silver Jubilee' began running over part of this line at previously unheard-of timings. Following the Castlecary accident in 1937, the company belatedly began fitting an electro-magnetic warning system to the Edinburgh–Glasgow main line, but the onset of war prevented its completion.

While this was a tacit acknowledgment by the LNER that drivers needed a supplementary system to confirm signal readings in the dark, and/or at high speed, they still had to do without. This particular line, which had experienced such horrendous accidents in LNER days in 1937, and again five years later, was not equipped with this important safety feature until 1958. (And even at that late date, it was the first Scottish main line to be so equipped.).

Neither the LMS nor the LNER were conspicuously heavy investors in their railway infrastructures, particularly when the huge turnover from the Scottish coalfields and the Glasgow suburban networks are considered. There was not one major station reconstruction in Scotland, no electrification, limited re-signalling, no constructive attitude towards branch-line traffic (except for underpowered steam railcars and investment in buses, and the latter was botched), and all these factors betray companies making do and reaping what they could from earlier companies' investments.

Labour historian, P.S. Bagwell went as far as suggesting that the investment in Britain's rail system between 1920 and 1938 totalled £125 million *less* than it should have been. Since he specifically excluded the Southern Railway from his criticism – he admired that company's electrification programme – the 'disinvestment' by LMS and LNER assumes even greater proportions.

Lord Monkswell could find plenty of material to support his case, yet when the companies were challenged during the General Strike, his lordship was to be found manning the signalbox at Marylebone. When Nationalisation was proposed after the Second World War, he argued strongly to preserve the very companies he had castigated for so long! Small wonder that, although he made good sense in his pronouncements on railway operation, Monkswell seemed unable to use his aristocratic status to influence absolutely anyone at all in the transport industry. One can't help thinking – more's the pity!

6

Joint Interests

There were seventy areas of Scotland where the LMS and LNER had shared interests. Three of these comprised joint railways – the Dalmuir, Dumbarton & Balloch, the Dundee & Arbroath and the Forth Bridge Railway. The first of these three came to be worked by the LMS rulebook, the second by the LNER's. The Forth Bridge Railway is described in more detail later, as is the Princes Pier line, in which both companies had an interest, but which was operated by only one of them.

Apart from obvious points of contact between the companies – Aberdeen, Carlisle, Perth, Stirling – there were a number of surprising conjunctions.

One small burgh where the LMS and LNER each owned a station, and where there was obvious scope for mutual economies, was Peebles, where locals could be forgiven for wondering if there was any railway co-ordination at all. A file in the National Archives of Scotland shows that Peebles was a focus of attention for both companies, and a name on the lips of the most senior members of railway staff.

This pleasant county town had one station operated by each company. In the 1860s, the NBR had taken over the locally promoted Peebles Railway, which was extended on to Galashiels and effectively became a 37-mile loop off the Waverley Route. In the same decade, the Caledonian entered Peebles from the west over the nominally independent Symington, Biggar & Broughton Railway, with that title summing up the route of the branch from the West-Coast main line.

Caledonian trains approached Peebles on what was surely one of Scotland's most scenic railway lines, crossing an attractive viaduct (which still stands) near Neidpath Castle, and then diving into tunnel before emerging at the company's station on the south bank of the Tweed. From the Caledonian station, a spur fifty-five chains (nearly 0.75 mile) in length crossed the Tweed and made a junction with the NBR in the Edinburgh direction. The spur line was not exactly overworked.

Peebles had been the subject of a ridiculous dispute in 1846, when both the rival companies tacitly acknowledged its perceived importance by agreeing to a conference to discuss how this strategic destination should be rail-accessed. After the 'Caley' had threatened to build a line south from Peebles to Innerleithen, and the NB had countered by announcing a line west from Peebles to Biggar, it was agreed that Peebles would be a geographical divider, with the CR operating west of there, the NB east of it. Ironically, at this time, neither company had any track within 20 miles of Peebles. Indeed, the NBR was still four months away from opening its first line, and the Caledonian had not turned a wheel anywhere!

Ten years after Grouping, the LMS and LNER could be forgiven for feeling that the traffic potential of Peebles had been somewhat overestimated.

Even at the height of the Edwardian era, the Caledonian had only timetabled four passenger trains daily each way, although the NBR station was busier. This was reflected in the 1931 traffic figures – 7,167 passengers booked by the LMS and 21,989 from the LNER station. (The latter company had already hastened to close Granton, with its 65,000 passenger journeys annually!). Despite the ratio at Peebles of three LNER passengers to every one on the LMS, the revenue figures were much closer – £2,383 for the former Caledonian station, £3,345 for that of the former NBR, suggesting that there may have been more booking for Glasgow or English destinations through Symington – and why not; even the 'Royal Scot' express stopped there (usually by request only, up to the Second World War, but at that time the Up 'Midday Scot' spent no less than 11 minutes on Saturdays at the now-vanished junction of Symington).

It is interesting to see that the LMS was prepared to rationalise its presence at Peebles to an extent that would have horrified the Caledonian negotiators of 1846. A joint study by the 'Big Two' in 1933 proposed that only full wagon loads, including livestock, would be dealt with west of the Tweed, with the LNER goods station handling all other goods and sundries. Passenger trains from Symington would travel right through the LMS station (specifically, *round* it, with the existing platform line removed) and terminate at the LNER station. Even the prestigious 'Tinto Express' would do this, its journey time to and from Glasgow being extended by 2 minutes for the extra fifty-five chains of its journey.

The LMS would be able to salvage its 60ft-turntable – not an insignificant saving. At the time, even an important rail centre like Stranraer, with heavy traffic from London and Glasgow by two different lines, had no turntable of such a diameter. (David L. Smith believed that the LMS was ordered by the Government to install a 60ft turntable at Stranraer, early in 1939, in anticipation of wartime traffic requiring more modern locomotives.).

In contrast, the LNER was muddling along at Peebles with a turntable no more than 42ft in diameter, which, with rails built to hang over the edges, could be 'stretched' to 2in short of 45ft! This was only sufficient to turn a Holmes D31 4-4-0; no Reid 4-4-0 could be accommodated. Since most passenger trains tended to run from Edinburgh to Galashiels via Peebles, and vice-versa, this was not a problem for the LNER, and the turntable was still in place in BR days. But in 1933, the LMS was quick to point out that it was operating locomotives which were 49ft in length over wheelbase into their station at Peebles. Midland compounds were a common sight here, despite their comparative newness, and were no strangers to the Dolphinton branch as well.

The detailed study of how to make economies in operating the two Peebles stations showed that the companies could co-operate when their interests were mutual, and the finished report went to both Sir Ralph Wedgwood on the LNER, and Ernest Lemon on the LMS. But the turntable problem surely killed any prospect of major reorganisation here.

For the LNER to have put in a larger table would have nullified any potential savings, and the LMS obviously felt that the Carstairs shedmaster could not be expected to withdraw Compounds and 'Dunalastairs' from working the branch when convenient. In addition – although it does not appear to be mentioned in the companies' records – it must have seemed illogical to have closed the spacious CR station, with its two platform edges, overall roof and avoiding line, to concentrate traffic on a single-line station, with no avoiding lines whatsoever. Even loco movements to and from the LNER shed would have to occupy the track beside this single, former NBR, platform, when passenger traffic permitted.

Even without mutual economies, Peebles's two stations survived into BR days. The former Caledonian station closed to passengers in 1950, and to freight some years later. The former NBR station lasted into the Diesel age, with closure coming in February 1962 to both passenger and freight. The possibility of trying a Glasgow (Central)–Hawick passenger service, with an engine-change at Peebles, appears to have been one leap of the imagination too far for the newly nationalised owners of *both* stations after 1948!

But rural bylines were not the only ones where the LMS and LNER sought to co-operate in securing economies. Records from the joint LMS/LNER committees now in the National Archives of Scotland, show that the solitary LMS clerk working at Edinburgh (Waverley) had no function, as late as the 1930s, except to answer any enquiries from members of the public seeking information about LMS services (in an LNER station!) and to purchase soap and towels for LMS trains leaving Waverley. This could refer to the three daily St Pancras departures over the Waverley Route, but these were LNER-operated for the first 98 miles. In the financial circumstances then prevailing, it is surprising that the post was allowed to remain in existence so long, especially since it cost £252 a year (in 1933). Of this, one and fourpence was spent annually on window-cleaning! The post was withdrawn from 1 February 1934.

Another surprising point of co-operation between the LMS and LNER in Scotland was in Greenock, on the Princes Pier branch. Because this had been authorised under the Clyde Navigation Act of June 1891, and known at that time as the Cessnock Dock Railway, its existence was guaranteed by the Caledonian, Glasgow & South Western, and North British Railways. Because of this unusual constitution it survived, as the Prince's Dock Branch Joint Railway, through the 1923 Grouping, and all the way up to 1948 when it was nationalised, along with the LMS and LNER. It was operated by the G&SWR until 1923, and by the LMS for the next twenty-five years, with passenger services finally ceasing in 1966. The nearest LNER railhead was many miles to the east, although the West-Highland line was just across the Clyde.

One of the first occasions when the 'Big Two' had to act in concert, after being established in 1923, occurred when the secretary of the Prince's Dock line intimated his retirement because of ill-health. As mentioned earlier, the individual concerned, James Ker, served two other 'paper' lines in a similar capacity, but they were both being absorbed by the LMS, and no replacement secretary was required for those erstwhile companies. The LMS Local Scottish Committee, which had the benefit of Caledonian representation early in 1923 (which was more than the LMS board of Directors could claim) took upon itself to appoint its own committee secretary to the part-time Greenock post, which carried an annual salary of £100. The LNER were informed that they would be required to pay 40 per cent of this sum, and this *fait accompli* was apparently agreed to.

The most illustrious Scottish railway concern to survive alongside the 'Big Two', right up to New Year's morning of 1 January 1948, was the Forth Bridge Railway Co.

In view of current media speculation about the future of this, the world's most famous railway bridge, it is surely worth looking at something of its history, particularly in relation to the twenty-five years between 1923 and 1948. It was not included in the Grouping because it was effectively a joint railway, with both the new LNER and LMS having a direct interest. The latter company's involvement might come as a surprise, so a little history should be recounted here.

Bridging the Forth was always going to be a nineteenth-century engineering challenge unlike anything ever seen before in the British Isles. Although the lowest estuary crossing, the distance to be spanned at Queensferry was over a mile, and the Admiralty insisted that there should be 150ft headroom at high water. The depth of the channel eliminated any possibility of a tunnel.

As the 1870s dawned, the NBR took the problem to its southern allies – the Great Northern and North Eastern on the East Coast, plus the Midland, which was planning to exchange cross-border traffic with the NB at Carlisle within a few years. A consortium called the Forth Bridge Railway (FBR) Co. was set up in 1873, getting off to an unfortunate start when its first board meeting had to be abandoned as inquorate.

Another unfortunate decision was the appointment of Sir Thomas Bouch as project engineer, and he planned a gargantuan suspension bridge, with supporting towers no less than 500ft-high, from which gigantic tubes would be suspended on chains. The tubes, 100ft apart, would each contain a single line of track. Work began in 1878, with foundations being dug for one of the towers on Inchgarvie island, in the middle of the traditional Queensferry passage.

Eighteen months later, in December 1879, a terrible storm did more than destroy Bouch's Tay Bridge, with the loss of seventy-five lives; it destroyed its designer's reputation. Within eight months, the FBR was asking Bouch if he would like to be relieved of his contractual obligations to them, while all work on the Forth was stopped, although not quickly enough to prevent the forging of the giant chains, for which Messrs Vickers had to be paid. Bouch demanded compensation for having his contract cancelled – was refused – and was dead within the year. The FBR shelved its plans to bridge the Forth for the foreseeable future.

But the English participants in the consortium – not so directly affected by the Tay tragedy – were made of sterner stuff, and demanded that the matter be reconsidered. This was done at a meeting in York in January 1881, the outcome being that the three English companies secured representation on the FBR board – it was surprising that this had not been the case earlier

– along with the appointment of two renowned engineers, Sir John Fowler and Benjamin Baker.

Fowler and Baker soon devised a cantilever design, based on traditional principles, and giving massive strength to what was basically a seamed viaduct running through the middle of the structure. The designers' philosophy was that, 'the successful engineer is he who makes the fewest mistakes'. Their design was sound, and with Sir William Arrol contributing the steel, the engineering was equally good. It had to be, as the Board of Trade, notoriously casual in its approval of bridges and railways hitherto, now insisted on a quarterly inspection of the works. There were to be no fewer than twenty-eight examinations.

The bridge took seven years to complete, being opened in March 1890 by the-then Prince of Wales (later Edward VII). With the help of its southern allies, the NBR now had an advantage of 29 miles over the Caledonian in operating Edinburgh–Aberdeen services, and twenty-one between Edinburgh and Perth. It had cost some fifty-seven lives, and continued to incur casualties even after opening. It meant closing the Granton–Burntisland ferry to rail vehicles, although passengers were still making that crossing, in the absence of a road bridge, well into the second half of the twentieth century.

The North British's contribution to the FBR consortium was 30 per cent, the Midland paying 32.5 per cent and the GNR and NER, 18.75 per cent each. The Midland's contribution was extremely generous. Once it began operating over Aisgill and into Carlisle in 1876, it soon discovered that there was barely enough traffic to justify a third Anglo-Scottish main line, particularly in winter. The NBR even demanded compensation for operating long-distance expresses over the Waverley Route – and the Midland paid! Yet the Scottish company had never hesitated to keep the Midland to its plan to build an expensive main line through the Pennines, and here at Queensferry we find the Midland Railway to be the biggest single financial contributor to the world's most expensive bridge.

All these constituent companies of the FBR had running powers over the Forth, although none ever used them except the North British. However, the North Eastern once threatened to, during a conflict with its northern neighbour! The NBR hurriedly settled on that occasion, rather than see NER green locomotives running into Perth (as they had a legal right to do)! The FBR company secretary and permanent way engineer posts were held by those in corresponding positions on the North British, and the LNER was to inherit this operational aspect of the partnership.

After 1923, the LNER appointed six directors to the FBR, with two from the LMS and two from the stockholders. In that first year, the LNER representatives comprised chairman William Whitelaw, the Duke of Buccleuch, Sir Frederick Banbury, Sir Frederick Fison, Lord Knaresborough and Sir Arthur Pease. The LMS was represented by Sir Ernest Paget and Alfred Wiggin. (Interestingly, the LMS 'Directors' Rolls' [i.e. diaries], which indexed board and committee meetings both by date, and under director's names, omitted Mr Wiggin's membership of the FBR board in the latter index. Let's hope he leafed through the other pages!). The quarterly board meetings were no longer held in Edinburgh, but usually at King's Cross or Marylebone, with the former specified for the 1923 meetings.

During the process of amalgamation, the new companies' solicitors came across a curious anomaly in the way the bridge was administered. The original Forth Bridge Act stipulated that the firm's directors must each own £200-worth of shares, but later legislation appears to have obscured this requirement without repealing it. In any event, the newer Act appeared to fall foul of the Companies Clauses (Scotland) Act, concerning directorial qualifications, which would still have required the directors to hold a personal financial interest in the company.

Despite this discovery in 1923, there is no record of the law now being complied with, and it appears that the LNER and LMS, effectively the owners of the Forth Bridge Railway, continued to administer it illegally, as had always been the case! (It would have been comparatively easy to assign shares to each director, just as the Caledonian Railway had done in its disputatious representation on the board of the Solway Junction Railway – the owner of another record-breaking viaduct in its time.).

The year 1923 also saw the publication of a technical survey by the Institution of Civil Engineers, which paid particular attention to the state of the track deck on the bridge. Effectively, the structure's three massive towers enclose a viaduct comprising two parallel ledges with transoms between them. These in turn support steel plates little more than one-quarter of an inch in thickness, suspended between the ledges. (This must have given food for thought as 125-ton Reid Atlantics hauled 350-ton expresses over the bridge with the dark waters of the Forth 150ft below!).

'From the maintenance point of view this type of floor is not favoured', concluded the report, and it was found that some of the rivets below the deck were worn down to 'pencil thickness' by stress and corrosion. Problems also resulted from the placing of the rails in continuous steel troughs, intended to minimise the effects of a derailment. A build-up of rainwater and grit in the troughs caused serious corrosion, but this problem may have been camouflaged by the use of conventional ballast on the bridge, and this was removed around the time of Grouping.

Accentuating any concern about maintenance was the growth in engine weights. The Institution of Civil Engineers study pointed out that Fowler and Baker had assumed the weights of engine and tender at no more than 77 tons. This was being exceeded as soon as the bridge was opened in 1890, and by the 1920s, Gresley's Pacifics were soon to take up duties north of Edinburgh, with a working weight of twice this amount. Indeed, by 1934 Gresley had designed the P2 Class for this particular route – all 160 tons of them! Meanwhile, the Bridge Stress Committee had reported, making clear that the crucial factor in deciding how much railway bridges could stand was the 'hammer blow' of piston within cylinder, not simply a locomotive's weight. With a Pacific or 2-8-2 distributing its weight on six axles, the Forth Bridge was effectively given a new weight rating, and continued to provide a vital transport link for its final twenty-five years in the ownership of the FBR.

A hazard which its builders could not have foreseen was the possibility of the destruction of the Forth Bridge by enemy action from the air. This first became a problem just twenty-five years after the bridge's opening, as eastern parts of the UK were subjected to Zeppelin bombing raids in the First World War. Scotland escaped comparatively lightly, the only raid occurring on a clear moonlit night in April 1916, when two of the German dirigibles were beaten off from Rosyth naval base – at that time home to Admiral Beatty's battle-cruiser squadron – by anti-aircraft fire. (The Zeppelins then attacked Colinton, Leith and Edinburgh, unfortunately killing eleven civilians, despite only attempting to bomb – by hand – military establishments and a dockland warehouse.). The bridge was reportedly being guarded by troops at this time, but the perceived enemy was not so much German, as Sinn Fein saboteurs. (For a summary of FBR defensive actions during the Second World War, see the relevant chapter of this book.).

The Forth Bridge is now once again in private hands (if non-profit making), its operators a frequent target for media criticism, as the traditional maintenance programme of 'three years of painting and then start all over again' seems no longer to be observed. New safety legislation has made maintenance much more difficult to accomplish in such dangerous conditions, and the structure may well have a finite life.

Two areas of commercial activity where the LMS and LNER learned to co-operate was in marketing. By the mid-1930s, tickets on certain

Anglo-Scottish trains on the East- and West- main lines were made inter-changeable: tourists from overseas, for example, could travel north from London on one line, and return by the other. 'Runabout tickets' were issued from centres where each company had an interest. In 1930, a tourist could purchase a week-long runabout ticket at Inverness for 15s 9d first-class, or 10s 6d third-class, allowing travel to Nairn, Forres, Elgin, Lossiemouth, Aberlour, Grantown-on-Spey, Carrbridge and Aviemore. Although Inverness was an LMS station, two of these geographical parameters were former GNSR outposts. The idea of being able to travel by steam power from Inverness on a circular route through Elgin, Craigellachie, south along the Speyside line, and back to the Highland capital – for little more than the 1930s equivalent of 50p – makes you feel you were born too late!

The companies also co-operated in the production of such publications as '*Scotland for the holidays*', from the mid-1930s. Areas of the country – the Lothians, Galloway and so on – were described purely from a tourist's view-point, with no emphasis whatever on which of the companies supplied the rail service in the area concerned. If the LMS and LNER were able to work together in this way, perhaps this begs the question as to whether a unified Scottish railway could have been established in 1923, after all – although it was Scottish railway interests, not English, who had opposed the idea!

7

Locomotive Policy

British Railways had not been in existence for more than two years post-war, before a programme of 'Standard' steam locomotives was announced. One short of a thousand were eventually constructed over a ten-year period up to 1960, intended to introduce a set of basic classes, enjoying many interchangeable features, and able to operate throughout the system. It was a logical idea, not perhaps carried out as well as it might have been, with some classes having no clear purpose, and with some designs showing misconceptions in detail. (Some LMS and LNER designs, such as the 'Black 5', and the B1 4-6-0s respectively, continued building after Nationalisation, but were clearly not part of any BR 'Standardisation' programme.).

But there was no such logic in the immediate locomotive policy of the LMS and LNER when new in 1923. True, the word 'standard' was bandied around when describing locomotive classes, but with no consistency. In 1925, LNER chairman William Whitelaw described the new marque of D11 'Director' 4-4-0s as an example of a 'Standard' class, when in fact they were nothing of the kind. These were built by Nigel Gresley, based on a pre-Grouping design for quite a different railway to the LNER's Southern Scottish lines (in fact, the Great Central), and to answer a motive power shortage – one more perceived than real – in one operating division only. The new 'Directors' were regarded by many observers, both then and in later years, as a tribute to J.G. Robinson, who had been a probable choice of chief mechanical engineer to the new LNER, and who later claimed to have recommended the younger Gresley.

The LMS later adopted the term 'Standard locomotive' in Stanier's time as CME after 1932. If Nationalisation had not intervened, all the remaining pre-Grouping engines – including the Midland 4-4-0s produced in such numbers from 1924 – would have been replaced by Stanier 4-6-0s, 4-6-2s, and 2-8-0s, as well as the Mogul designs by Ivatt, one of Stanier's successors. There were to be 17 standard classes in all – quite a contrast to the 400 or so inherited from the constituent companies – and the LMS official history seems unsure of the exact number!

Before proceeding farther, the renumbering of Scottish locomotives in 1923 should be mentioned. On the western system, the Midland was undoubtedly the dominant member in motive power, with no renumbering. The Scottish companies were allocated five-figure numbers from 10,000, as if to emphasise their distance from the centre of the LMS universe! On the east, it would certainly appear that the North Eastern Railway's stock was the 'core sample'. None of that company's 2,156 engines were renumbered; all other companies' locomotives were. In the case of the North British, 9,000 was added to existing numbers, while the GNSR had 6,800 added.

Curiously, the numerical superiority of North Eastern Railway locomotives in the new East-Coast company does not seem to have influenced the choice of a braking system. While the two major constituents of the LMS, the LNWR and Midland, used the vacuum brake, making its adoption inevitable in 1923, the LNER had to make a choice on the matter of braking. The NER had used the Westinghouse brake, as had the North British and the Great Eastern. However, the Great Northern, Great Central and GNSR utilised the vacuum brake, and this was the system the LNER adopted for its passenger trains, plus the small minority of freight trains which were fitted with a continuous brake (mineral trains were not, their brakes being applied by hand).

The adoption of the vacuum system created a logistical problem, with three Westinghouse-fitted locomotives to every two employing vacuum. Nevertheless, the conversion programme went ahead, no doubt with Nigel Gresley's approval as the former GNR chief mechanical engineer. Doubtless, he could claim that this would make it easier to operate services linking with the LMS, without having to use specially adapted, dual-braked, stock such as that used previously on the East Coast and Midland/NBR services. Of course, this was effectively to allow another line to dictate the LNER's technical policies, and in his three-volume work on the history of the LNER, Michael Bonavia is highly critical of this decision. He believed that the vacuum brake took too long to release after an application, pointing out that a special exception had to be made for the former GER lines to enable Liverpool Street suburban services to continue working with Westinghouse, and thus maintain time on the tightly scheduled 'Jazz' trains.

Effectively, the vacuum system required a vacuum to be pumped out of the train hoses every time the train required to restart; in other words, the system had to be activated just to release the brakes in the first place.

Perhaps the main attraction of the vacuum system was that it incorporated a 'fail-safe' principle in the case of the brake pipes being fractured, or a train breaking in two. The loss of vacuum automatically applied the brakes in such an instance. In 1929, a film called *Flying Scotsman*, starring Ray Milland, featured exactly this – an express with its rear coaches detached and threatening to catch up with the first section – something which was impossible when the vacuum brake was in use. Gresley was reportedly furious at such an inaccuracy, and swore never to allow film companies on LNER property ever again!

'Cascading' is a process as old as railways themselves. All the pre-Grouping companies carried on the practice of relegating express passenger locomotives to stopping trains after a few years, or reallocating them to secondary routes. Finally, after a longer period, what was once the pride of the main line could be found pottering along local branches. Freight locomotives were luckier, working at the same level in the operating hierarchy for what might prove to be decades on end.

When motive power cascading took place within a pre-Grouping company, where there was a fair chance of the footplate staff being fully aware of what was happening in the company's locomotive department, and information about the peculiarities of individual classes was easily exchanged among crews, this process was understood and not a particular source of complaint. But it was a different story in the new super-companies.

Some of the immediate transfer of locomotives from south to north in both LMS and LNER defied everyday wisdom. (Incidentally, there seemed to be little or no transferring of Scottish motive power to south of the border, indicating that the 'cascade' was invariably northbound.). These transfers will now be examined.

The former North British had a fine stud of 4-4-0 locomotives, probably quite sufficient for all the passenger rosters on the system apart from the Edinburgh–Aberdeen and Waverley Route expresses – and those could be handled quite adequately in the meantime by the Reid Atlantics. There were three types of Reid 4-4-0s available for main line traffic. The 'Scotts', with their imaginative names (*Jingling Geordie, Wandering Willie*) handled most of the passenger traffic, particularly on the Edinburgh–Glasgow main line. The 'Intermediates' were a mixed-traffic design, equally at home on fish trains (among the fastest workings on the system) and express passenger.

The 'Glens', originally designed for the West Highland line, were so successful that they were built in sufficient numbers to make them commonplace working in Fife and the Borders.

So, with this excellent crop of 4-4-0s available to the LNER, what did the managers of the new company do? They introduced yet more 4-4-0s.

The first of these were the Great Northern D1 Class, known popularly as 'Ponies'. Whether they were popular with the footplatemen is another matter, Norman McKillop's autobiography giving a rather different impression. Within five years of Grouping, Nigel Gresley introduced two more classes of 4-4-0 on to the former NBR system. Both the D11s and D49s were new-builds, although the former was a fairly straightforward version of the Great Central class designed by Robinson. This was a strange choice for a hilly rail system.

Although reasonably well-thought of by their crews, the Scottish-based 'Directors' were described by McKillop as 'a little high in the wheel', and this was no exaggeration. Their 81in-driving wheels were greater than the new A1 Pacific, and were only to be equalled by the prestigious new 'Royal-Scot' design over on the LMS ! It is difficult to see the logic of such an engine being introduced anywhere except on the Edinburgh–Glasgow route, and the extra diameter of the driving wheel would hardly help in climbing Cowlairs incline. Indeed, it was a D11 which caused four deaths in 1928 when it was unable to lift a 150-ton load (the equivalent of five empty coaches) up this very incline.

The 'Shire' Class of 1927 was scarcely much better, and these units were regarded as rough-riding. Surprisingly, these were a genuine Gresley design, but again, the driving wheel (80in) was not particularly practicable for the Scottish system, and lessened the engine's potential for mixed traffic. Working a D49 on a Glasgow–Edinburgh express was voted 'The mad hour' by St Margaret's men; the riding qualities of the design can be guessed at from this description.

In retrospect, greater numbers of six-coupled locomotive classes such as K2 and K3, would have proved a better long-term investment, supplementing the native 4-4-0s, particularly the 'Intermediate', with its ability to haul either passenger or freight.

The swelling of the ranks of 4-4-0s on the Southern Scottish Area inevitably triggered a 'cascade' within Scotland, with a number of former NBR 4-4-0s – and by no means the more recent of them – being moved to the Northern section. Such old warriors as the D31s, originally introduced by Holmes in the final years of the nineteenth century, found themselves working on the Elgin and Deeside lines out of Aberdeen after 1925, when they themselves were replaced by the ex-GNR 'Ponies'. Admittedly, the comparatively modest weight of the D31 made it a suitable subject for transfer to the GNSR, and no fewer than twenty-seven of the class made the trip northwards. Since many of them were to eventually return to former NBR lines, where they continued to work up until 1950, their own displacement by the 'Ponies' is made to appear ever more inexplicable.

The native motive power which they were gradually replacing on the new Northern Division was a range of 4-4-0s used equally for both passenger and freight work. These comprised no fewer than eleven classes, which the LNER classified as D38 to D48. Some of these had been designed by William Cowan as far back as the 1870s, but the latest of them, the D40s, had been charged with express work between Aberdeen and the Highland Railway nucleus of Inverness. One of the latter class, *Gordon Highlander*, is now preserved.

There was to be another transfer to the Northern Division which were even more surprising than that of the former NBR D31 – namely the move of 25 Great Eastern B12 4-6-0s, which began a lengthy migration to former GNSR lines in April 1931. This was an inspired idea, giving an extended working life to locomotives already displaced from leading East Anglian services by Glasgow-built B17s. The former GER engines had a low axle-loading, but their arrival in the north seemed to surprise Inverurie works, now responsible for their maintenance. Following the introduction of more stringent livery rules in the summer of 1928, Inverurie was only maintaining mixed-traffic and freight engines, which were painted lined and unlined black respectively, so the B12s, although working express duties, gradually lost their green liveries in pre-war days.

For a different view on stock cascading, one turns to the immensely enjoyable writings of David L. Smith. The late Mr Smith recorded the locomotive workings of the G&SWR and its lines under LMS ownership, in a series of chronicles which represents a record of loco working unique anywhere in the UK. In his book on the G&SWR in LMS days, he is honest enough to admit that he would have welcomed cascading in 1923! Commenting on the profusion of powerful engines on the LNWR, he wrote, 'surely they could spare us a few to run our trains more efficiently' – forgetting that most Scottish lines had a more restricted loading gauge, requiring them, as he imaginatively put it later, to have a haircut and shave!

It soon became clear to him that, if there was to be a 'cascade' of motive power to the former G&SWR, it would largely consist of 'rejects' that

Caledonian shedmasters no longer wanted. So badly organised was the rationalisation – if it can be called that – of motive power on the 'South West' by the mid-1920s, that only two superheated locos were available for Anglo-Scottish express workings south from St Enoch, while the Caledonian line had no fewer than seventy-nine available. Indeed, the 'poor relation' status of the SW lines were betrayed by many of its express workings being hauled by non-superheated engines, an unhappily unique achievement by this time, with Gresley Pacifics operating on the rival LNER.

Even when Midland Compounds were introduced on to services on the former G&SWR system, their allocation was apparently achieved by pep-perpot. Corkerhill, the Glasgow depot with duties down the Ayrshire coast, as well as to Carlisle, received only two, while various small depots received an equal allocation, and one engine went to Hurlford, which had no express rosters whatsoever. While most enginemen respected the 'Compounds', and Mr Smith was no exception, they were 'too high in the wheel' (81in) for lines such as Girvan–Stranraer. Of twenty-eight incidents in the early 1930s where Mr Smith had recorded trains slipping to a stall in section on the Swan's Neck, a notorious incline in the middle of the Wigtownshire moors, no fewer than twenty-four were attributable to the use of 'Compounds'.

Ironically, the LMS policy of super-elevating curves to increase downhill speeds on these Wigtownshire banks made uphill work that much more dif-ficult. It all added up to a picture of decision-making on locomotive matters taking place many a mile from the site of operations.

Two other new types introduced to the area by LMS management in the 1920s were the Midland 2P – a 'simple' version of the 'Compound' although lighter and less powerful – and the Horwich 2-6-0 'Crab', a nick-name Mr Smith disliked. He believed that these Moguls were ideal for the South West's mountainous routes, but rostering changes meant that they had to undertake more long-distance runs, including tightly timed sec-tions north of Ayr. He believed that engines on Glasgow–Stranraer services could have been changed at Ayr, with the Moguls operating south of there, but management wanted greater mileages on paper, and the 2-6-0s shook themselves into the repair shops. Meanwhile, the 2Ps, willing and popular engines, were given an unrealistically low loading capacity in official docu-ments, leading to their being removed from services they were perfectly capable of operating. Again, here was every sign of decision-making being carried out without reference to local footplatemen.

On the Highland section of the LMS's Northern Division, there was no immediate replacement of Highland Railway motive power. Indeed,

O.S. Nock, on a visit to the north in 1927, commented that, 'the whole line north from Glasgow and Edinburgh to Wick, Thurso, and Kyle of Lochalsh was solidly pre-grouping in its locomotive power'. He believed that the motive power mandarins of Horwich and Derby held a high opinion of Highland engines, and, 'all were agreed that they looked well in Midland Red'.

One major development by the LMS was the reintroduction of the 'River' Class to the former Highland metals, for which these handsome 4-6-0s had been designed by Frederic Godfrey Smith in 1915. Unfortunately, the six engines, badly needed at that time of heavy passenger and coal traffic serving the Grand Fleet at Scapa Flow, proved unacceptable to the line's civil engineer. This precipitated the wretched Mr Smith's resignation, while his employers cheerfully sold the engines on to the Caledonian – for more than the Highland had paid to build them! It was a bargain for the 'Caley' too, and that company extracted some good work out of them for some twelve years before new research findings of bridge stress conditions allowed the 'Rivers' to return to the line they were designed for. (Incidentally, O.S. Nock wrote that if Smith had been more diplomatic in his handling of the 1915 rejection of his locomotives, he, and not Stanier, might have become chief mechanical engineer of the LMS!).

Other Caledonian types, including Pickersgill's 4-4-0s, were to be seen on the Highland section, but few LMS-designed types found their way north of Inverness before the ubiquitous 'Black 5' began to make its way northwards.

It would be wrong to imagine that the new 'Grouped' companies exclusively looked on their Scottish constituents as dumping grounds for their worn-out engines. The best example of an early positive locomotive introduction came about at Haymarket shed, Edinburgh. In 1924, the foot-platemen there, later to be known as the 'enginemen elite', received their first Gresley Pacifics. A legend was born.

Haymarket operated these locomotives, whether A1, A3, or A4, for up to forty years, and soon came to be regarded throughout the system as a 'Gresley' shed. When in later years, the first of the Gresley Pacifics to be rebuilt by Edward Thomson was allocated here, nobody south of the border was surprised when it was soon sent packing back south again. Similarly, members of Peppercorn's later A1 Class, were only allocated to Haymarket when the class was virtually complete, and tended to be somewhat underused by the depot, frequently found pottering along the Perth line or Waverley Route with a six coaches. In contrast, Gateshead invariably rostered an

A1 to a northbound overnight sleeper service, so that the southbound 'Flying Scotsman' was nearly always A1-hauled on the northern part of its journey.

But in 1924, the arrival of the Pacifics in Edinburgh caused some surprise. Since it had been moved to Roseburn from its site near Haymarket station thirty years before, the depot, still known as Haymarket, had housed North Eastern Railway express locos to operate Anglo-Scottish expresses over the entire Newcastle–Edinburgh route, even although the fifty-eight miles north of Berwick was part of the NBR (indeed, the first part of that company's mileage to be constructed). For operational reasons it was found convenient to station NER locos at, initially, St Margaret's, and then Haymarket after 1894, with their crews finding accommodation in Edinburgh.

The arrangement seemed to work reasonably well, but there may well have been a feeling among the former NER authorities that, in terms of express passenger operation, Haymarket was merely a sub-shed of Gateshead. If that was the case, it was soon dispelled, with the first of the new Gresley Pacifics, being built by North British Loco in Glasgow, being allocated to Edinburgh. Indeed, Haymarket received five before the first of the new build was sent to Gateshead. Nevertheless, their crews thought of them as 'North-Eastern' engines simply sub-shedded in Edinburgh, an attitude which had some justification with former NBR men at Haymarket rapidly having to catch up by 'learning the road' south of Berwick.

Interestingly, in 1928, when the LNER introduced non-stop running on the 'Flying Scotsman', it was felt that only North-Eastern Area locomotives could operate the service from the northern end, and a wholly unnecessary transfer of three A1s took place from the Tyneside depots of Gateshead and Heaton to Haymarket. One of these, No.2580 *Shotover*, headed the first southbound 'non-stop', receiving a hero's welcome of truly tumultuous proportions on its arrival at King's Cross – probably the highlight of this comparatively obscure engine's career!

Within six weeks, the operating authorities acknowledged that the transfer of NE-based Pacifics to Edinburgh had been unnecessary (and was causing an engine shortage on Tyneside), and when the train was challenged to a race with an Imperial Airways Argosy aircraft on 15 June 1928, it was a Haymarket engine which represented the railway at the head of the 'Flying Scotsman'! (And was the winner too, although that's not how the press reported it, or how the Royal Aeronautical Society recorded the outcome! The reader is referred to this author's book *Non Stop!*).

This long-distance service was crewed by men from King's Cross, Gateshead, and Haymarket (former NER men only, to begin with) for the first twelve summers, so Tyneside played a key role in the running of the non-stop 'Flying Scotsman' right up until the outbreak of the Second World War. The Gateshead crews involved had to work a tenuous roster involving three nights in succession away from home, but seemed perfectly happy to do it, obviously believing that they were the men with the best knowledge of the northern half of the train's itinerary. Small wonder then, that the initial allocation of No.2563 and its sisters to Haymarket, may have come as something of a surprise, but it was a farseeing decision, and with its crews eagerly undertaking duties as far south as York, Haymarket would soon match Polmadie for its ability to run Anglo-Scottish expresses to the highest of operating standards.

The introduction in 1928 of Gresley's A3 – a refinement of his A1 – meant that Haymarket had a new marque of the line's finest express engines, and the sight of Pacifics crossing the Forth Bridge became a daily one. Dundee and Eastfield (Glasgow) depots received the original locomotives allocated to Haymarket in 1924, although not until 1937, in an internal cascading process which was very welcome to depots operating trains wholly within Scotland. Carlisle (Canal) was another shed which was introduced to the idea of operating Pacifics, although two of its acquisitions were in fact new. Indeed, one of them, No.2749, never operated from any other shed after running in at Doncaster. This explains the arcane legend scrawled among the graffiti at King's Cross by a frustrated rail enthusiast hoping to see every one of the A3s – 'Died waiting for *Flamingo!*'

John Thomas described his first view of what one of his friends called 'a big American engine' (interesting, in view of the A1's supposed legacy from the Pennsylvania RR K4 of 1915). Hurrying to the lineside one day in 1924, Mr Thomas was able to view the new No.2563 *William Whitelaw* climbing Cowlairs Bank towards him: 'I had a vision of a great boiler with a bulge in it, an incredibly small chimney, and bowler hats bobbing on the footplate'.

If there were Pacifics at Haymarket from 1924, and at Eastfield, Canal, and Dundee within the next thirteen years, what was to be found at Polmadie and Corkerhill to operate expresses across the border? As we have seen, Corkerhill fared badly from the LMS's curious allocation policy, but nevertheless that depot found itself rostering its top link crews (and its only two superheated G&SWR engines, Nos 128 and 129, renumbered as 14673/4 by the LMS) on a duty which included the 10 a.m. south from Glasgow Central, a service soon to be named the 'Royal Scot'. It was a strange roster for a depot with few 'Compounds' and with crews having to hurriedly 'learn the road', particularly when Polmadie could boast 'Dunalastair' 4-4-0s and a stud of massive 4-6-0s, all operated by experienced and capable crews.

What Polmadie did not have in the mid-1920s were post-war six-coupled express locomotives comparable in size and power to the new 'racehorses' on the East Coast. The handsome Pacifics being turned out to Gresley's design at North British Loco in Glasgow in 1924/25 were despatched eastwards to Edinburgh and beyond, while Polmadie found itself operating new 4-4-0s even smaller than the 1890s 'Dunalastair' Class!

Not until 1927, four years later, did the West-Coast main line receive its first post-war class of six-coupled express engines, and Polmadie acquired six of them. These were of course the 'Royal Scot' Class, built, and to a considerable extent, designed, at NBL Glasgow, also the birthplace of twenty of Gresley's Pacifics in 1924. (As well as some of the Southern Railway 'King Arthur' Class. It only remained for the GWR to order some 'Castles', and NBL could have boasted the full main line set!).

The 'Royal Scots' were built in what O.S. Nock described as 'a shipwreck hurry', but still missed the launch of the 1927 summer holiday season. Already, the LMS management had realised that the imposition of the Midland 'small engine' policy, intended to handle comparatively light loads, was not really practicable on a main line running some 540 miles north from Euston. Inevitably, the hastily assembled 'Scots', after early impressive performances, proved to be heavy on coal and repairs, and would not realise their full potential until re-boilered by Stanier from 1943 onwards. At least Polmadie received six of the class: when Stanier's streamlined 'Coronation' Pacifics began to emerge from Crewe from 1937, they were allocated to Western Division depots for at least two years before it was decided to entrust any of these lovely engines to the LMS's northern (i.e. Scottish) cousins!

Corkerhill, as we have seen, received no 'Royal Scots' when new (or later in LMS times either). Ironically, members of the class based at Leeds (Holbeck) later did some of their best work on the 'Thames–Clyde Express' over the G&SWR route; the author, brought up in a suburb of Edinburgh where Gresley's Pacifics went past in a blur, could not believe his eyes when on holiday in Dumfriesshire, viewing the daily spectacle of an immaculate 'Scot' (rebuilt by this time) pull up at Annan (population of 4,000) and then restart and pull up *again* because the train was too long for the platform!

Meanwhile, the railway companies' ability to construct locomotives in Scotland came under severe review. The LNER effectively terminated construction at Cowlairs (Glasgow) and Inverurie not long after taking over, although both continued to undertake heavy repairs on all but the Pacific express engines the company was to introduce. (In fact, Cowlairs overhauled Gresley Pacifics for the first few years after their introduction into Scotland in 1924.). The LMS continued new building at St Rollox until 1924, with repair work being transferred there from Kilmarnock (G&SWR), and Lochgorm (HR). Indeed, Kilmarnock works was partially demolished in 1929, eight years after constructing its last locomotive.

Scottish nationalists could reasonably point out that such English plants as Crewe, Derby, and Horwich continued to build from scratch on the LMS, while the LNER maintained new construction at the former works of GNR, NER, GER, and GCR – all, in fact, except the Scottish factories.

While it was certainly true that Cowlairs had never built anything as large as a 4-6-0 or 2-8-0, a number of the new classes sent to Scotland, for example the D11s and D49s, were 4-4-0s anyway, and the latter's boiler was used on the J38, a Gresley 0-6-0 design which was hardly ever seen outside Scotland. Ironically, St Rollox had built more large locomotives than Derby ever had and, in a double irony, both companies, along with the Southern, did not hesitate to make use of Glaswegian expertise at North British Loco when ordering new builds such as the LNER A1 Pacific and B17 4-6-0, and the LMS 'Royal Scot'.

The last locomotives built at a Scottish railway company works for either of the 'Big Two' was an order for twenty Class 60 4-6-0s to William Pickersgill's Caledonian Railway design, completed in 1924. These were not universally well liked – indeed, they were called 'Greybacks', not a compliment in Scotland – but one of them tested well on the West-Coast route south of Carlisle, and David L. Smith believed they had the potential to be very good engines indeed. Whether good or not – and E.S. Cox has pointed out that by 1948 this class was the only one on the LMS never to have cracked a mainframe – they brought to an end a tradition of Scottish railway companies building their own locomotives, a custom which went back eighty years.

Curiously, the historian John Thomas, in writing his chronicle of the Springburn area of Glasgow, minimises the effect of Cowlairs and St Rollox losing their engine-building role. He quotes management figures, showing that it cost nearly £50 more to construct a boiler at Cowlairs than at Doncaster, and this appears to have nipped any combined union complaint from both Cowlairs and St Rollox in the bud. Future complaints – in the former NBR works at least – appear to have been targeted against Thomas Heywood, works manager, after transferring from Inverurie. 'At least a steady flow of repair work was assured', concludes Mr Thomas.

If Gresley's Pacifics had made a huge impression when they came to be shedded at Haymarket in 1924, that was as nothing when the Edinburgh-born chief mechanical engineer's latest design arrived from the south ten years later. This was the P2 2-8-2 design known as 2001 *Cock o' the North*. With its four sisters, this massive locomotive with its predatory front end was believed to be the only British eight-coupled ever designed for express passenger work. (For rivals, one had to visit the miniature R&ER and RH&D railways, or count in the 2-8-0s designed for the Somerset & Dorset.).

The passenger work targeted for working by these giants was Edinburgh (Waverley)–Aberdeen via Dundee. It is a main line cursed by heavy gradients, usually straight off the platform ends as at Aberdeen and Inverkeithing (both southbound), or Dundee in either direction. There is curvature equalled only by that on the Waverley Route, and even a single-line section. Yet the traffic had always been heavy, since the LMS (former Caledonian) route proceeds southwards through Strathmore and Perth, only turning Edinburgh-wards from Larbert, missing Dundee. In addition to serving Dundee, Scotland's fourth city, the LNER line also traversed the Fife coalfield, Kirkcaldy – one of Scotland's largest communities – but also connected with St Andrews, the important university town and golfing resort.

While visually impressive, the P2 was always going to present its operators with a problem, as its lengthy wheelbase could create difficulties in the negotiation of yard trackwork. Super-heaters and the smokebox saddles also proved difficult to maintain, particularly in wartime conditions, and a P2 'failed', for either of these causes was unable to make its way to Cowlairs under its own steam, for obvious reasons. Once there, it appears that the works were unable to handle the problem – much to the disappointment of Haymarket shedmaster, Geoffrey Lund – and the rebuilding of the class became inevitable by the mid-1940s.

There was also the question of the huge firebox, which the Edinburgh driver, Charles Meacher, believed, 'in America would have been fed mechanically'. He went further on this point, arguing, 'When opened out, No.2001 was beyond the capability of one fireman to sustain'. Of course, the comfort of footplate crews never bothered designers or managers over-much (although Gresley was reported to be having qualms of conscience on this point towards the end of the 1930s).

1 Anglo-Scottish expresses via Carlisle and the Waverley Route required co-operation between LMS and LNER as they inherited the former Midland and North British Railway services from London (St Pancras) through the Midlands and the Pennines, and then over the Waverley Route to the Scottish capital. Here, LNER A3 No.2748 *Colorado* is seen accelerating past the wayside station of Hassendean, heading south to Carlisle with the 12 o'clock noon departure from Edinburgh for London, probably around 1932. (Robert Clapperton Agency)

2 An unusual example of Anglo-Scottish co-operation in locomotive engineering is represented in this 1930s view of LNER 4-6-4 No.10000. Designed by Edinburgh-born Nigel Gresley, it incorporated a high-pressure Yarrow boiler, and is seen here at Tweedmouth heading south on an Edinburgh–Newcastle service. The locomotive was later rebuilt in streamlined form, and was rarely seen in Edinburgh thereafter. (Robert Clapperton Agency)

3 A streamliner at Symington. Not yet repainted in anonymous black, one of the LMS 7P Pacifics nevertheless manages to hide its identity as it slows to a stop with a southbound express in August 1942. It is probably No.6225 or No.6229 as the livery is red with gold speed lines, and the chimney is single. This modest Lanarkshire station was visited by many named trains over the years, including the 'Royal Scot' and 'Midday Scot'. (Montague Smith)

4 The LMS 'Crab' 2-6-0 was hardly a handsome machine, but was popular with enginemen, and worked on the LMS and BR Scottish lines through five decades, well into the 1960s. This wartime picture from 10 August 1944, shows the footplate crew and guard posing with Peebles (West) station porter, Mrs Aitken. The wife of an LNER signalman, this lady deputised for a male staff member transferred to the West-Coast main line for the duration. On the right can be seen Peeblesshire forestry products, destined to become pit props. (Montague Smith)

5 Not much more powerful than the later Caledonian 'Jumbos', the LMS 4F nevertheless enjoyed a higher nominal power rating. No.4191 is seen here at Biggar on 2 August 1938. (Montague Smith)

6 The 'Black 5' was one of the most numerous and successful locomotive designs of all time. A mixed-traffic 4-6-0, it worked throughout the LMS system in Scotland, from Stranraer to Thurso. No.5466 is seen at Peebles, carrying a Carlisle shedplate. (Montague Smith)

7 The LNER goods workhorses included the J36 0-6-0, originally the NBR class C. Here, No.9687 is seen with its dual brake fittings – for both vacuum and Westinghouse – visible on the front buffer beam. When this picture was taken in 1936, this locomotive was a mere forty-four years old, and would reach seventy before withdrawal by BR in 1962. (Montague Smith)

8 Operating locomotive turntables by hand was a reality almost until the end of steam on BR, so it should come as no surprise to see a crewman bending his back (on right of the picture) to turn former CR 4-4-0 No.14500 at Peebles on 27 August 1937. This turntable was installed in 1906 to handle locos working into Peebles in connection with the Royal Highland Show – whose 1926 location at Kelso caused the LNER major headaches. The clerestory-roofed coach on the right is believed to be part of the 'Tinto', working to and from Glasgow. (Montague Smith)

9 This fine Montague Smith picture of a Pickersgill 4-4-0 at Peebles has been published before, but is particularly interesting as this late 1930s picture shows the 60ft-turntable that was so central to discussions between the LMS and LNER about Peebles rail services. The owning company required tables of this size elsewhere (principally at Stranraer) but the LNER table was too short to accommodate LMS engines such as this, and Midland Compounds, if the traffic had been pooled as proposed in 1933 (see the chapter 'Joint Interests'). (Montague Smith)

10 Now preserved in its original CR livery, No.14010 is seen on shed early in the 1930s, when it was used by the LMS to power officers' specials. It was, of course, originally CR No.123, built for the Edinburgh Exhibition in 1886, and distinguished by its efforts heading the 1888 'racer' from Carlisle to Edinburgh in record time. It is now preserved in the Glasgow Museum of Transport. (Montague Smith collection)

11 The Caledonian 'Dunalastair I' class was already some thirty-five years old when the LMS was formed, and unfortunately, none of them survived the 1930s. Here, No.14319, one of the first of a 'dynasty' of 4-4-0 power, is seen at Slateford on 8 October 1926. (Montague Smith)

12 A Caledonian 4-6-0 class designated by the LMS for freight haulage was the 179 class, rated 3F. Here, No.17905 is seen in the late 1920s, with its wingplates removed and new safety valves, but retaining its surprisingly roomy cab. (Montague Smith)

13 Super-power on the LMS. Two former CR 903 class 4-6-0s double up on a
southbound train out of Aberdeen in the late 1920s. The leading engine is No.14754,
a sister engine to the famous *Cardean*. Both are equipped with eight-wheel 'water-cart'
tenders, necessary because of the lack of water troughs north of the border until the LMS
installed three sets. (Montague Smith)

14 The culmination of the 'Dunalastair' classes was the 4, of which No.14452 was an
example. Built from 1904, they proved highly durable and some survived ten years into
BR days. This express consists of a curious combination of non-corridor and express stock.
Note the eight-wheel tender. (Montague Smith)

15 Another view of a 'Dunalastair 4', showing the later appearance of the class in LMS days – in black, with no company crest, and with the number on the cab side. The early LMS policy of showing the engine number on both smokebox door and tender could lead to problems if a tender swap was necessary! (Montague Smith)

16 A Pickersgill successor to the famous 'Dunalastair' series of CR 4-4-0s, No.14472, awaits departure from Peebles with a train for Biggar. Note the roses in the flower bed in the foreground, looking good in this 4 September 1940 picture. Not many amateur photographers in wartime were allowed to produce a camera in a railway station or yard without being reported to the police, and this period was one when 'fifth columnists' were particularly feared. It says much for the reputation of Montague Smith, that he was able to continue railway photography throughout the Second World War, and this book is all the richer for the illustrative record he produced. (Montague Smith)

17 The LMS inherited a number of important docks from the Caledonian so, not surprisingly, it also inherited dock 'pugs'. Here is one of them, No.16028, seen at Balornock in Glasgow in July 1945. The design appears to have originated with the Neilson company in Glasgow, and the LNER Y9 'pug' is not dissimilar. Both companies frequently coupled these engines to a wooden tender. (Montague Smith)

18 Carstairs depot as seen on 11 August 1936. In the foreground is Midland Compound No.1068, although this engine was in fact built new by the LMS in 1924. In the background the former G &SWR mogul No.17826 can be glimpsed, probably having worked in over the Muirkirk line with a train from Ayr, and receiving attention at Carstairs, where a wheel-drop could be undertaken. (Montague Smith)

19 The Midland Compound locomotive was highly thought of by engine crews and traffic managers alike, but whether it was worth building such small engines for express duties when the LMS was new in 1924/25, was doubtful. Here, No.1136 is seen on the turntable at Peebles on 29 August 1938, its presence in this pleasant railway backwater perhaps a sign that main-line expresses were now too demanding for such a 4-4-0. (Montague Smith)

20 In 1931, the LNER decided to transfer a number of former Great Eastern locomotives, such as this B12 No.8524, to the Great North of Scotland lines, where some of them operated for more than twenty years. This particular locomotive bears an experimental water-feed apparatus on top of the boiler, giving inevitable rise to the nickname 'Hiker', and is seen on an Aberdeen-bound express at Portnockie in 1938. (Montague Smith/ National Archives of Scotland)

21 The pride of the old North British Railway was the Atlantic class, introduced from 1906. This is the last of the class, out-shopped in June 1921 and named *The Lord Provost*. The LNER numbered it 9510, and it is seen here at Glasgow (Queen Street) on 24 April 1935, with the driver, Robert Thomson, in the cab. (Montague Smith/National Archives of Scotland)

22 The Caledonian had been absorbed by the LMS for less than a year when this picture of Dunalastair IV, No.14442, was taken near Stirling in June 1924. Believing that its shareholders were being short-changed, the 'Caley' remained independent in the first half of 1923, although such associated lines as the Cathcart District and Callander & Oban joined the LMS at that time. (J. & C. McCutcheon)

23 This 1949 shot of a Drummond 0-6-0 (ex-CR and LMS) contains a number of puzzles. The locomotive is being watered so it is presumably in use, but lacks a front-coupling chain, has a shedplate where the numberplate might be expected in BR days, and sports the number 47239. As it is clearly not the official No.47239 – a Midland 'Jinty' tank engine – it looks as though there has been a misunderstanding about BR's renumbering policy, or someone was having a laugh! The stovepipe chimney was no joke though. (Montague Smith)

24 Although taken in June 1924, this photograph of a Stirling–Oban goods, shows a Drummond 0-6-0, No.587, still in CR livery. As made clear in the text, neither the LMS nor the LNER was to invest much in their freight services over the next twenty-three years. (J. & C. McCutcheon)

25 A fine picture of a 'Small Ben' No.14400 *Ben More*, seen at Elgin in September 1927. The combined sandbox and front driving-wheel splasher is pure Drummond, although in this case, the designer was Peter Drummond and not the better-known Dugald. To its credit, the LMS intended to preserve one of these attractive machines, but BR thought otherwise. (J. & C. McCutcheon)

26 Elgin was one of the most important burghs on the Aberdeen–Inverness route, which saw an element of joint working between those pre-1923 enemies, the Highland and Great North of Scotland railways. The station in this 1920s picture is Highland, with the GNSR station off to the right. (J. & C. McCutcheon)

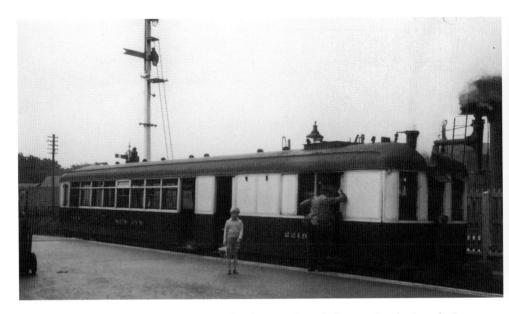

27 In the later 1920s, the LNER attempted to improve branch-line services by introducing steam railcars built by the Sentinel company of Shrewsbury. Their novelty value helped to generate impressive returns initially, but the cars did not age well, and were underpowered for Scottish operations. The vehicle seen here is shown at an English station (Whitby), but these cars operated in the Edinburgh and Aberdeen areas, as well as on the former Forth & Clyde Junction. (J. & C. McCutcheon)

28 Boat of Garten Station, seen here in a June 1933 postcard, is still open to the public on the preserved line from Aviemore. The station nameboard instructs passengers to 'change here for the LNER line', although this was effectively an end-on junction between the former Highland Railway (LMS) and Great North of Scotland (LNER). At this time, a 'rover' ticket issued at Inverness would allow unlimited travel for a week in this area for the modern equivalent of 50p! (J. & C. McCutcheon)

29 The largest GNSR class of locomotives inherited by the LNER was the D41 4-4-0, and this example, No 6899, is seen on an express working near Cullen on the coast line. This particular engine operated out of Keith for most of its life, which lasted for no less than fifty-six years. (J. & C. McCutcheon)

30 The transfer of no fewer than 25 B12 locomotives to former GNSR lines by the LNER made good sense. With an engine weight of only 63 tons, carried on five axles, these handsome engines from the former Great Eastern lines provided useful – but lightweight – power options to traffic managers in the North East. (J. & C. McCutcheon)

31 One of the new classes introduced to Scotland by the LNER was the D49 4-4-0, of which No.2755 *Berwickshire* is an example, seen at Eastfield, Glasgow. Designed by Sir Nigel Gresley, these engines had massive driving wheels, which made them unsuitable for the kind of mixed-traffic duties which became their usual rostering. (J. & C. McCutcheon)

32 The J39 0-6-0 class, introduced on to LNER metals by Gresley from 1926, was something of a throwback to earlier times when freights were expected to be hand-braked. At least this class could handle passenger trains when required, and the author once enjoyed a footplate trip on a J39 on the Langholm branch. (J. & C. McCutcheon)

But it is surely unarguable that some locomotive designs – and the LMS 'Duchess' could join the P2 when this point is made – failed to fulfil their operational potential because manual firing was insufficient to allow the boiler to reach full thermal efficiency. Incidentally, Mr Meacher records that the P2 'was capable of singeing hair and overalls', with the fireman having to provide the necessary gloves at his own expense. One wonders what the footplate union was doing about all this.

Haymarket in Edinburgh, and Polmadie in Glasgow, were the only Scottish depots during the lifetime of the LMS and LNER, to operate the two classes of locomotive which represented the acme of express steam operation over the border. These were the Gresley A4 and Stanier 'Princess Coronation' Pacific locomotives, built from December 1936 in the case of the LNER engines sent to Scotland, and 1937 in the case of the LMS. The first streamliner to be allocated to any Scottish depot was No.4483 *Kingfisher*, sent to Haymarket in time to take up duties on Boxing Day 1936. She was followed within the next three months by three more avian-themed loco-motives, *Falcon*, *Kestrel*, and *Merlin*. Only the third of these was to remain at the Edinburgh shed, but the stud was increased with the introduction of A4s built in 1937 to power the 'Coronation' express, and these were named after constituent parts of the Empire.

This particular working was of course very short-lived, and the best work undertaken by the Haymarket A4s was the operation of the non-stop expresses ('Flying Scotsman' – 1937-38 and 1948, 'Capitals Limited' – 1949-52, and 'Elizabethan' – 1953-61) between Waverley and King's Cross. By the 1950s, Haymarket settled down with an allocation of seven streamliners, all of which were fitted with corridor tenders, although the most frequent performers from the north end tended to be *Merlin* and the (now preserved) *Union of South Africa*. The former achieved nearly seventy non-stop journeys in the year 1960 – hauling a near 400-ton load daily on a prestige service when already in its twenty-fourth year – while the latter Pacific achieved the fastest–ever journey between the capitals, as related later in this book.

While the A4 was unchanged before 1948 – apart from the permanent removal of the valancing over the driving wheels during wartime – the Stanier engines emerged in both streamlined and un-streamlined forms. The first batch of the latter were Nos 6230-34, all named after Scottish aris-tocracy (as was the streamlined No.6229), appearing first in single-chimney, and then double-chimney form, and all eventually fitted with massive smoke deflectors. The latter addition is believed to have been hastened following the deaths of the crew of No.6231 in the Ecclefechan collision of 1945 (see the chapter 'Accidents').

At first the LMS would not allow these superb engines out of sight of Euston, it seems, and it was only during wartime that they were eventually allowed to cross the border to be assigned to Polmadie. The distribution of the class reflected the need for express passenger power on other services, in addition to the 'Coronation Scot' and 'Royal Scot', but in practice, there were simply never enough of these engines on the West-Coast main line during the days of steam power. (Incidentally, the class was usually referred to as the 'Duchess' Class, although twice as many of its members were named after British cities served by the LMS. Poor old Aberdeen and Dundee missed out, however, despite surely being just as important as two English cities which were honoured – Lichfield and Carlisle.).

The A4s never operated from any Scottish shed except Haymarket in LNER days, although, displaced by Deltics from 1962, they found their way northwards onto former LMS services between Glasgow (Buchanan Street) and Aberdeen. One might have expected these to have been operated by the 'Duchesses', now also displaced by Diesel power on the West-Coast main line, and familiar to footplate crews used to operating former LMS types. All this was some fifteen years after the LMS and LNER had ceased to exist, but the 'Duchess' design limitations proved to be their undoing. Intended to operate between London (Euston) and Glasgow (Central), on a line with eleven sets of water-troughs, their tenders lacked the capacity to allow them to stray onto such lines as Glasgow–Perth–Aberdeen, where there were no troughs at all. O.S Nock, oddly but accurately described the class as, 'very thirsty things'. Consequently, the A4s, with their extra 1,000 gallons of water in their tenders, operated expresses well into 1966, outlasting most of their unfortunate LMS rivals by some three years.

As the 1930s wound to their end, no one class of locomotive dominated the Scottish lines of the LNER, but on the LMS, the 4-6-0 was king. When photographing trains from the lineside, Patrick Ransome-Wallis once admitted that he would often lower his camera as yet another train hove into view headed by a 'Black Five'. Ubiquitous was certainly the word to describe these mixed-traffic locomotives, which numbered 842, and were found throughout the LMS system in Scotland from Stranraer to Thurso. After Nationalisation they colonised a number of former LNER lines as well, particularly the West Highland, while this author remembers a Carlisle (Canal) engineman saying that he would rather take a '5' on the Waverley Route than the (more powerful) Gresley V2. Charles Meacher recalled cheerfully preparing to leave St Margaret's on a '5', when the shedmaster told him to abandon 'that great Caley thing' and take a run-down K3 instead. Such was the persistence of pre-Grouping values!

Interestingly, the LMS sister class of 4-6-0, Stanier's 'Jubilee', although 'higher in the wheel' to use a Norman McKillop expression, was more often seen on former G&SWR tracks, particularly on the hilly Stranraer routes, whether from Glasgow or Carlisle. But these two classes, together with the numerically inferior 'Patriots' and 'Royal Scots', meant that 4-6-0s made up a high proportion of haulage of all passenger and braked goods trains in LMS days – and for a long time after.

In his memoirs of work in the LMS, chief mechanical engineer's officer, E.S. Cox, recalled that, around 1933, a Class 4 4-6-0 was proposed for operation on the company's Scottish lines. This would appear to go against the whole ethos of standardisation, namely the production of locomotives which were easy to maintain, utilise interchangeable parts, and, above all, be able to operate on any part of the system. The Class 4 would have an exceptionally light axle loading of 15.75 tons, but have little power advantage over pre-Grouping types. Although twenty-one were scheduled for construction in 1934/35, the CME's team was able to persuade their civil engineering colleagues north of the border to simply strengthen their bridges, and soon 'Black 5s' were operating over the former Callander & Oban.

Braked freights on the LMS were just as likely to be hauled by a '5' as anything else, although the 'Crab' 2-6-0, dating from the mid-1920s, was a popular locomotive, and Stanier's 8F 2-8-0 began to make its mark in the years before the war. Indeed, this locomotive was adopted as a standard by the War Department early in the conflict, some of them built by, and working on, the LNER while awaiting shipping abroad. As war conditions soon demanded a cheaper and simpler heavy-duty locomotive, the 'Austerity' 2-8-0 and 2-10-0 Classes were produced, largely to the design of R.A. Riddles, of the LMS. So many of these were built by NBL in Glasgow that one of them was given the name *North British*, and they were to be found over much of the Scottish system in BR days. (Interestingly, one of each wheel classification was tried out on a passenger train rake between Dumfries and Kilmarnock in BR days, the 2-10-0 coming out very much on top. The LMS corridor tender was used during these tests, in June 1952, the company initials still proudly displayed.).

Of course, un-braked goods trains made up the bulk of traffic in steam days, and these were always in the charge of the workmanlike 0-6-0. The Caledonian had furnished the LMS witharound 150 of these 'Jumbos', and both the G&SWR and Highland contributed their own examples, some of the latter surviving the war. The post-Grouping addition was the former Midland 4F – an uncomplicated engine which failed to develop the breed

The LNER added two 0-6-0 Classes to the three it inherited from the NBR. (There were actually seven such classes, but those in LNER Classes J31 to J34 were approaching obsolescence.). The North British passed on what became the J35, J36, and J37 Classes, all of them good for daily mineral workings right into the 1960s. Indeed, the last steam engine to operate in normal conditions in Scotland was a J36 0-6-0, when in its sixty-eighth year! (As one of the most recently built members of the class, it actually lasted some ten years *less* than some of its fellow J36s.). Gresley supplied Classes J38 and J39, the former being almost entirely based in Scotland, and arguably the only transport contribution the LNER made to the coal industry in Fife and the Lothians. In contrast, the J39 frequently undertook passenger work, particularly in the south of Scotland. The author once enjoyed a footplate trip on a J39 hauling the Langholm branch train; it was only later that the tendency of the J39 to derail, and roll over, was read about!

While not as numerous, or as celebrated, as its LMS 4-6-0 counterpart, the 'Black Five', the LNER's B1 was a useful workhorse seen on most of the system. Although introduced eight years later than the '5', it had a more old-fashioned appearance, with its parallel boiler and flat-cab front. This simply underlined the brilliance of Stanier's design, but the B1 could claim a war-time birth – in 1942 – and was an amalgam of available parts and affordable costings.

The first forty of so of the class were named after species of springbok – a happy choice of name (apart from *Bongo*) since a B1 in good nick was regarded as one of the fastest accelerating locomotives around. Only two 'antelopes' worked regularly in Scotland – *Chamois* and *Klipspringer* – but a number of later engines named after LNER directors operated out of Edinburgh, Carlisle (Canal) and Glasgow, with such B1s as *Strang Steel* and *Murray of Elibank* continuing the North British tradition of distinctive Scottish names. Meanwhile, the Northern Division petitioned for increased turntable capacity in 1945, specifically so it could operate B1s.

Two LNER locomotives which were definitely non-standard were the sole representatives of the V4 Class, designed by Sir Nigel Gresley in 1941 with the West Highland line very much in mind. With the first of the two being officially named *Bantam Cock* – the unofficial name for the second engine should not tax the imagination overmuch – these were almost a lightweight version of a V2, and were well-thought of by their crews. Unfortunately, Gresley, in his final year of life, was criticised for designing such comparatively expensive locomotives at a time when there was a national need for 'Austerity'-type power. Indeed, Edward Thompson, Gresley's successor, introduced the highly successful – and much cheaper – B1 within a year.

In 1947, both companies began to tinker with the possibility of introducing Diesel-electric power to their main lines. While the LNER produced, and approved, a plan for no fewer than twenty-five such locomotives to operate on the East Coast, with their principal base in Edinburgh (see chapter 'Towards Nationalisation'), the LMS actually got down to building two such engines. This involved the construction, at Derby, of Nos 10000 and 10001. Incorporating English Electric equipment, they provided an opportunity of operating long-distance express services without intermediate stops, since they could be connected to the train by gangway. They were undoubtedly powerful when working in tandem, and almost the equal of a 'Deltic' in horsepower when working together. However, the state of trackwork probably prevented these units from fulfilling their full potential in the years immediately after their construction in 1947; as we have seen in the chapter on Anglo-Scottish services, Nos 10000-01 were still constrained by an official 60mph-ban, in places, even as the 1950s dawned.

These engines were frequent performers on Euston–Glasgow services, proving capable on test of achieving an 800-mile return journey in less than twenty-four hours for days on end. Two Stanier 'Duchesses' (Nos 6256-57) were built by H.G. Ivatt in 1947/48 with such technical innovations as roller-bearings and improved firebox arrangements, all designed to improve the engines' ability to undertake lengthy rosters with a reduced 'turnaround' time, and thus, directly compare Diesel with the most up-to-date steam design.

In fact, there seems to have been little in the way of formal testing to compare the respective merits of the two types of motive power, and it was in a Glasgow newspaper's correspondence columns, in January 1948, that the 'rivalry' received a detailed airing. A Mr Menzies wrote to the *Herald*, strongly backing the Pacifics, pointing out that the Diesels could only equal one of their steam rivals if coupled together, whereupon their combined weight was 50 per cent more than that of a 'Duchess' Pacific, while their length was twice as great, possibly necessitating a reduction in the number of coaches hauled. Interesting points these, but Mr Menzies had bestirred a formidable opponent.

Cecil J. Allen was visiting Glasgow in that first week of 1948, along with O.S. Nock, to lecture to Scottish schoolboys on the wonders of the modern railway system. (What kids would attend this kind of thing nowadays?). Mr Allen also wrote to the paper, taking up cudgels on behalf of 10000-01, and pointing out that their greatest advantage was in their guaranteed availability. Perhaps he was premature – the whole point of constructing an improved version of the 'Duchess' was to investigate whether technical improvements could increase steam locomotive mileage, and the new BR administration do not appear to have prosecuted the comparisons as thoroughly as the LMS had been preparing to.

Detailed results would have been interesting: as it was, what mileage figures emerged were inconclusive. The two new Pacifics, with their modifications designed to lengthen annual mileages, ran approximately 5,080 miles a month (No.6256) and 4,070 (No.46257). In comparison, the unmodified No.6240 accomplished 6,018 miles a month. No 'Duchess' achieved more than 90,000 miles annually, not even the last two, intended to reach 100,000 annually. In contrast, the two Diesels are recorded as having notched up 50,000 miles in three months, creditable indeed when their availability figures could be affected by staff unable to remedy minor problems, the equivalent of which would not 'fail' a steam locomotive.

As a matter of interest, A4 No.60009 ran a higher mileage than any of its LMS rivals (1,850,000 miles approximately) at an average of 5,530 miles monthly. It enjoyed some three years more 'life' than the 'Duchesses', but this reinforces the theory that the LMS Pacifics, in being retired too early, never delivered to their full potential.

As it was, the Diesels could achieve one thing which a 'Duchess' could never do: they hauled the 'Royal Scot' non-stop on 1 June 1949. In addition, the comfort of the Diesel cab would be an eye-opener to LMS crews. E.S. Cox recorded that 10000 'rode like a charm from the first day'.

In a letter to the author, Alan Robinson, a member of the electrical section of the CME's department at Derby, tells of a cab ride from Glasgow southwards on the 'Royal Scot' working: 'We were checked all the way from Eden Valley [just south of Penrith] to Crewe. All the same it was some ride!' Although a steam enthusiast, Mr Robinson recalls how his department were determined to outshop at least one of the Diesels before the LMS lost its identity on 1 January 1948. 'They are the only Diesels for which I have any affection' he says. Obviously, he viewed the London Midland & Scottish in the same light.

Finally, almost as a footnote, it must be recorded that, of the 'Big Two' operating in Scotland, only the LMS can claim to have had much of an eye for posterity in locomotive matters. That company permitted two historic locomotives to be preserved in store at St Rollox – the unique Caledonian 4-2-2 No.123, and the Highland Railway 'Jones Goods' 4-6-0, after both were withdrawn from traffic in 1934/35. One could wish that more had been preserved – a Whitelegg Baltic tank from the G&SWR, for example, but in fact none of that pre-Grouping company's stock survived under LMS auspices. (The locomotive now representing that company in Glasgow's Museum of Transport was rescued from industrial usage in the 1960s.).

But this was more than the LNER managed. Despite interest shown by Sir Nigel Gresley, attempts made to preserve a Reid 'Atlantic' fell victim to war preparations in 1939, and no representatives of NBR or GNSR loco-motive studs were conserved by the LNER. It was left to BR to perpetuate the gamboge with *Glen Douglas* in 1959, but the Great North's 4-4-0 *Gordon Highlander* only survived after BR Scottish Area board gave way to an enthusiasts' campaign and reversed a 1957 decision to scrap this out-standing example of the GNSR locomotive stock. Since then, the Scottish Railway Preservation Society has admirably helped to fill the gaps.

8

Anglo-Scottish Express Trains II

At Grouping, the new LNER had inherited from the Great Eastern Railway a contract to operate Pullman Cars for the next seventeen years. Transferring them to the more lucrative East-Coast main line proved a good business move, and the 'Harrogate Pullman' was the result. In 1925, it was decided to extend this service to Scotland, the new train connecting King's Cross with Leeds, Harrogate, Newcastle, Edinburgh (Waverley) and, from 1927, Glasgow (Queen Street).

Departure from Edinburgh for the south was scheduled at 08.30 a.m. at first, but the later decision to start the train from Glasgow involved a 10.05 a.m. departure from Queen Street and 11.15 a.m. from Waverley. As this left an unsatisfied need (only recently and belatedly perceived by management) for an early-morning service to the south, a new express was introduced in 1928, leaving Edinburgh at 07.40 a.m. Picking up at Dunbar, it was recorded as averaging forty-five passengers travelling daily in its first six months. Unfortunately, and despite these figures being less than impressive, this introduction impacted on the loading figures for the Pullman, Maj. Stemp informing Calder late in 1928, that, 'patronage for the retimed Pullman has fallen considerably since the introduction of the later working'.

In the following year, the title 'Queen of Scots' was bestowed on the train, and it was to run in this form until 1964, apart from in 1939-48. While presumably aimed at a business clientele, one has to wonder how many businessmen (or women) could afford to spend up to nine-and-a-half hours sitting in a luxury train, with, needless to say, no means of contacting the office! It was simply a more comfortable version of the already ponderously timed trains on the route; the best part of a decade would pass before this company, and its rival to the west, attempted to combine luxury with celerity.

Also introduced on the LNER in 1928, on 24 September, were sleeper services for third-class passengers. This inevitably increased loads – and the ratio of tare weight of trains to the weight of passenger and luggage was already running at 10 to 1 – but with sleeper trains, even greater tare weights have to be hauled to incorporate sleeping passengers. On the Waverley Route, a successful trial with an A1 Pacific in October of that year meant that 400 tons could be hauled without assistance, 110 tons more than that allowed for the Atlantics. Two such Pacifics were expected to be operating by 18 December 1928, presumably out of Carlisle Canal depot, although the files are silent on that point. On the Edinburgh–Dundee section, an extra 80 tons could be handled by Pacific haulage. At least it was all worthwhile – bookings at Aberdeen for points south were reported as heavy from the start, with demand exceeding the number of berths.

British railway companies were hardly at the forefront of streamlining in the early 1930s. Numerous examples were in service in the United States, Germany, and even in the Japanese mainland colony of Manchuria, before all four of the Grouped companies in the UK began to look at the concept.

Streamlining had benefits which were both practical and economic. By reducing the air resistance to any moving vehicle, fuel can be saved, or speed can be increased without a similar rise in the amount of fuel consumed. There is, of course, publicity value to be considered, and there is no doubt that streamlining was a 'sexy' concept in the 1930s, with, in American examples, industrial designers imposing their visions of air-smoothing on locomotives which had previously been entirely functional in both design and operation.

A streamlined locomotive first crossed the border late in 1935, when the spare A4 at Gateshead, ready to deputise if a failure occurred on the up 'Silver Jubilee' express, gained some revenue-earning mileage by running a later Leeds–Glasgow service from Newcastle as far as Edinburgh. Locomotive No.2511 *Silver King*, was the silver-liveried engine in question, although it was to be less than two years before her (his?) blue-liveried fellow A4s began more regular operations north of Newcastle. Before going on to examine the 'Coronation' and its LMS counterpart, a closer look at this morning express from Leeds is worthwhile.

In 1935-36, the service heading north from Leeds at around 8.30 a.m. conveyed a vehicle almost unique in British rail history. This was a specially customised cinema car, equipped to show commercial cinema films to audiences of up to forty at a time on route. Curiously, the film (16mm) was projected back-to-front, with the projectionist *behind* the screen, on which the image naturally appeared the correct way round. Charles Gregory, an employee of the Pathé company, worked for a year on this train (named the 'North Briton' in 1949), his shift allowing him three hours in Edinburgh, while the coaching stock made its way to and from Glasgow (Queen Street) without him. Mr Gregory was expected to work Sundays if the cinema was required on excursions, but was allowed three days off per fortnight. When asked if this moving cinema was well-patronised, particularly on an early-morning service, he advised this author that he was hardly in a position to know, being isolated in his compartment with his Debrie projector, and would only be advised to start the performance when a steward at the other end of the coach pressed an electric 'doorbell'. Later, the coach was transferred to Leeds–London services, and eventually led to a career for its operator in the Ministry of Information.

History records earlier uses of cinema cars in the UK – the LMS showed films on its 1929 non-stop run from Glenboig to Euston – and there was an isolated use of such a vehicle on the LNER in 1924. But the 1935 cinema service is thought to have been the only occasion when a vehicle was customised to show cinema films on the move.

As far as the Scottish operations of the LMS and LNER are concerned, streamlined passenger train services did not cross the border until 1937, and curiously, they arrived on exactly the same day – 5 July 1937. The rail companies were aware that air services between London and Scotland were about to become commonplace – they certainly should have known about this, since both companies had invested in Railway Air Services. As this author has concluded in his book *Streamlined Steam*, both LMS and LNER completely overestimated the efficiency and marketability of air travel at the time. The 1930s technology of airline passenger transport was unbelievably crude by modern standards – un-pressurised aircraft, grass airfields, passengers seated in cane chairs (certainly in 1929) – and the railways already offered luxurious travelling facilities in comparison.

But air travel was exciting and newsworthy, with every false claim and downright fib originating from the airlines being reported faithfully by the drooling press. For example, in 1928 Imperial Airways announced that they could introduce a London–Edinburgh service that would cut five hours from the train's journey time. The 'Flying Scotsman' was certainly some ninety minutes too slow even at that time, but when a trial 'race' took place, starting in London, with A1 No.2563 heading the express, the air travellers failed to reach Waverley Station before the train. Not only that, but in 1935 the RAS airline adopted a schedule not far short of six hours for a London–Glasgow service – rather more than the 210 minutes claimed for this kind of distance by Imperial Airways in 1928, and never put into effect in the next twenty years. (Ironically, the LNER had powers to operate air services to 20 degrees east of longitude – see the chapter 'Off the Rails' to see what that could have entailed.).

So the threat from the air was more imagined than real, but the LNER in particular pushed ahead with its plans for a streamlined express service in 1935. We should be grateful that they did, for although the resulting trains were all withdrawn by the outbreak of war in 1939, the locomotives which powered them, Gresley's A4 Pacifics, were still operating into the mid-1960s, while their LMS rival, the 'Duchess' Pacifics, had an undeservedly shorter working life. Both classes were a delight to the eye of every railway enthusiast.

The first LNER – indeed, British – streamlined express was of course the 'Silver Jubilee', running once each way daily between King's Cross and Newcastle. Its luxurious silver stock was not seen north of the border until 26 September 1936, when a trial run was made between Newcastle and Edinburgh (Waverley). Being a Saturday, this meant that the 'Jubilee' set could be used, along with a dynamometer car. If the intention was to test the practicability of a two-hour schedule between Newcastle and Edinburgh, this experiment succeeded, with the northbound journey taking a record 117 minutes. Southbound, the run was accomplished in one minute less, with an estimated 2,600hp being generated on Cockburnspath bank – 4 miles at 1 in 96.

Four days later, the LNER management in Edinburgh acknowledged a memo from Sir Ralph Wedgwood detailing a programme of repositioning 'distant' signals, to allow greater time for express trains to brake from high speed. (A 'distant' was a semaphore signal with a yellow arm indicating whether the 'home' signal – the next to be reached by the train – was likely to be at danger or clear.).

None of the signals to be re-sited were in Scotland, but it would surely have been appropriate for the company's Scottish management to request some of their signals to be included in the programme. In the previous November, a test on the Edinburgh and Grantshouse section of the ECML, and between Edinburgh and Glasgow, had shown that a number of signals were not capable of slowing, and then stopping, a fast-moving train, particularly at Falkirk, Linlithgow, and Dunbar. One can only assume that the LNER had not fully circulated its plans for a streamlined Anglo-Scottish express, even as late as September 1936. Indeed, the earliest proposals being considered by planners closer to King's Cross featured a London–Aberdeen service in 9¼ hours. Otherwise, a more positive response to the Wedgwood memo should surely have emanated from Scottish Area HQ.

Train operation on Cockburnspath bank had already occupied the Scottish Area management of the LNER in 1931. It became necessary to install new signals almost halfway up the bank, in order to eradicate delays to southbound traffic, as any train stalled or winded climbing the Berwickshire incline would force a train held at Cockburnspath to tackle the climb virtually 'cold'. This was leading to a 'domino effect' of stalled trains requiring assistance from Dunbar, with consequent delays.

James Calder authorised £1,023 expenditure to insert new automatic signals halfway between Cockburnspath and Grantshouse signalboxes, to be operated entirely by track-circuiting, and not even requiring telephone communication between the boxes. If the circuit covering the lower part of the bank was clear, then a train could enter it from the north, while an earlier train completed its climb to the summit, protected by a signal triggered at danger by the broken current on that half of the bank. It was such a simple system that it is puzzling that it had not been introduced earlier. The LMS was to introduce similar signals at Auchencastle and Harthope, effectively dividing the two block sections of Beattock incline into a total of four – again, the technology of track-circuiting had been available for the best part of fifty years, and could have been applied appropriately.

In the event, Scotland welcomed two glamorous new services on the same day, 5 July 1937. The LNER's contribution was the 'Coronation', linking King's Cross and Waverley in six hours, with a 4 p.m. departure northbound and 4.30 p.m. going south. Over on the west, the LMS introduced the 'Coronation Scot', scheduled to link Euston and Glasgow (Central) in six-and-a-half hours, with a 1.30 p.m. departure from each station. Both train titles marked the crowning of George VI on the previous 12 May. Ironically, the start of the annual visit of the new royal family to Holyroodhouse – always in the first week of July – deprived the rail companies of much-needed newspaper publicity for the launching of these new trains.

The operation of the 'Coronation' was extremely challenging, requiring an overall average speed of 67mph, on a train which regularly comprised nine coaches. This included two guard's vans, two kitchen cars and an observation car. With all the stock being fitted with dynamo belts, which had an infuriating habit of working loose, the 'Coronation' was not an easy train to operate, especially in winter when no locomotive had ever before worked the near 400-mile journey without change.

While locomotive failures on this train occurred approximately once in every thirty-three journeys, there were some excellent performances to compensate. Perhaps the best throughout the length of the 393-mile journey was that achieved by No.4488 *Union of South Africa* on 25 August 1939. Leaving King's Cross eight minutes late, after powered points had been affected by a summer thunderstorm, the Haymarket Pacific, driven by its London and Tyneside crews (who changed over at York), reached Waverley punctually. This gave a 352-minute time – an estimated 340 minutes net – for the run, at an average speed of 67mph including two stops, surely a record for a steam-hauled train over such a distance, and with two coaches more than the marginally faster (non-stop) run between Euston and Glasgow by LMS No.6201 *Princess Elizabeth* three years previously.

The record set by No.4488 occurred barely a week before the service closed as the war clouds gathered. But this coruscating run should not be allowed to obscure the fact that the 'Coronation', powered by Haymarket and King's Cross locomotives, was a daily achievement, accomplished on a main line infested with slow-moving freight and mineral traffic, and with semaphore signals throughout almost the entire route – and with no cab-signalling to confirm the drivers' reading of the road ahead. As for the firemen, it has been estimated that each one of them on the 'Coronation' roster was expected to shovel thirty hundredweights of coal per hour, while regulating water supply to the boiler, bringing coal forward from the rear of the tender towards the end of the journey, and assisting the driver with signal sighting at any time during the shift. The LNER was very well served by these men.

When considering the LMS streamlined service, the 'Coronation Scot', admiration is tempered by the fact that the train did not have specially built stock, nor was its schedule particularly challenging. The latter point was a major disappointment, since the 1936 run already mentioned, by *Princess Elizabeth*, had been carried out to test the practicability of a six-hour schedule, and it certainly succeeded in that. However, the locomotive would have been 'failed' overnight under normal circumstances, the northbound journey causing a problem that required all-night repairs in Glasgow before the special could head off south again. Yet the 'Coronation Scot' was granted an extra 45 minutes for the journey. Nor was the stock new, with the exception of two Brake Firsts and Corridor Firsts in each of the three sets assembled for the service, including one spare rake. In other words, of the twenty-seven vehicles provided for this crack service, only six were new. This really was cheese-paring to a major extent.

Yet everything else about the 'Coronation Scot' was outstanding. The locomotive bore a US-style streamlined casing which, from a distance, gave the new 'Princess Coronation' locomotives a bullet-like appearance. With Caledonian blue as the livery chosen for both locomotive and train, the visual effect was irresistible, enhanced by the use of silver speed lines from the engine-front, continued right along the coaching stock. (Incidentally, the use of Caledonian blue – and the purists argued about how authentic it was – hardly featured in the publicity for the new train, and was changed to Midland red with gold speed lines without compunction in little more than a year.).

The train even had its own tune, composed by Vivien Ellis. It was still being used by the BBC to introduce the Paul Temple radio series for many years after the war and, of course, after the train had ceased running. With the LMS pulling out all the stops to publicise the service, Scotland could boast a very impressive addition to its express services. But the reality was a little different.

Scotland's National Archives contain a unique copy of a log of every run undertaken by the 'Coronation' during its service between July 1937 and August 1939. The loading figures recorded are disappointingly poor; in the first week of the service the down 'Coronation' was arriving with only around fifty passengers sprinkled throughout its nine-coach length.

Here, the LNER was reaping what it had sown. If the 1896 protocol had been torn up at Grouping as it should have been, the company would have had the best part of fifteen years to foster and encourage more regular journeys between Edinburgh and London among the business community in both cities.

Not only that, but because the train service had been so dilatory for nearly forty years, and because of a rigid fares structure, rival transport concerns flourished in linking the two biggest Scottish cities with London. The East-Coast company could not even kill off the coastal shipping trade for passengers; in his recent autobiography, historian Paul H. Scott recalls taking a steamer from Leith to London as late as September 1932. Long-distance bus services had sprung up in the previous decade, their operators unable to even advertise a time of arrival, so technically primitive was the service! Matters improved; they were being advertised to take sixteen hours from London–Glasgow by the early 1930s.

As an alternative, a same-day journey between Glasgow and London in seven-seater American-built Hudson Super 8 cars was on offer from travel agents in Buchanan Street at that time. Needless to say, bus, and even car, offered a cheaper alternative to the train, which, before 1937, could not claim all that much superiority in terms of journey time either.

There was even something perverse about the timings of the two rival streamliners. While the LMS appears to have been satisfied with the turnover of its 'Coronation Scot', the train's 1.30 p.m. departure time occupied the traditional channel of the 'Corridor' (later the 'Midday Scot'), which was a slow, almost omnibus service, making numerous stops. It was popular with holidaymakers and casual travellers. The new service, stopping only at Carlisle, and then very briefly, was simply creaming off those who were travelling throughout, but the slower train still followed behind, offering as many as six stops. In other words, if the 'Coronation Scot' had left Euston and Glasgow at, say, 4.00 p.m., it would have been *generating* new business.

Additionally, the northbound streamliner's arrival time of 8.00 p.m. in Glasgow, brought little advantage to any traveller who lived outside the city. Central was not a through station, certainly not for long-distance trains, but had (and still has) an excellent suburban network, with commuter trains running into the late evening to connect with any later arrival time.

Interestingly, over on the LNER, the 'Coronation' might have benefited by 'swapping' its departure times with the LMS service! While patronage south of Newcastle was good in both directions, there was no immediate demand for a late afternoon London–Edinburgh service – the idea of a businessman travelling south by a overnight train the previous night was hardly encouraged when, traditionally, there had been no train northwards the next day after 1.30 p.m. or thereabouts. The down 'Coronation's arrival at Edinburgh at 10.00 p.m. connected with only two main line trains – one each to Glasgow and Kirkcaldy – thus failing to take advantage of Waverley's impressive selection of northern destinations such as Aberdeen, Dundee, Perth, and St Andrews, which a 7.30 p.m. arrival could have afforded. Is it possible that the LNER might have re-timetabled the 'Coronation' if war had not intervened? A lunchtime departure time should have been reconsidered, or an extension of the route to either Aberdeen or Glasgow (Queen Street).

It seems unarguable that the 'Coronation' was a disappointment in commercial terms, and is lost to public memory. Its loading figures were poor, the observation cars failed to capture the public's imagination and its press launch was muted. When this author mentioned the 'Coronation' in a recent newspaper article about Sir Nigel Gresley, an irate reader wrote to the editor denouncing me for failing to research the subject properly. The only 'Coronation' on Britain's railways was the Stanier Pacific of that name! Why couldn't I get my facts right? Unfortunately, the editor of the *Edinburgh Evening News* published this rant, so it seems that the LNER's flagship express from the 1930s really has vanished without trace!

The Second World War affected the four Grouped railways to a major extent, exhausting them in terms of manpower, investment and maintenance. The streamlined expresses were withdrawn even before war was declared, and the 'Royal Scot' and 'Flying Scotsman' became semi-fasts. Not surprisingly, the war's effects required a solution which was far-reaching, even to the extent of bringing private ownership of Britain's railways to an end. Just as the First World War gave rise to legislation invoking the Grouping, so the Second World War produced Nationalisation. (For a brief history of the LMS and LNER in Scotland during 1939-45, see the relevant chapter.).

While Britain's railways suffered from the effects of bombing, this was less of a problem in Scotland than farther south. What affected the railways more severely, in the longer term, was the reduction in track maintenance, and rolling-stock renewal. The figures were worrying – track repairs were undertaken at only 70 per cent of pre-war figures, resulting in a two-year backlog by the end of the war in 1945. Not surprisingly, a 60mph speed restriction was in place nationally. As for rolling-stock, the LMS constructed only sixteen new vehicles a year during the war – this for a company with a stock of more than 22,000! Locomotive overhauls and heavy repairs were greatly reduced, owing to the companies' works undertaking the production of war material.

Inevitably, the timetabling of Anglo-Scottish expresses was relaxed to even more than the bloated times allowed under the 1896 agreement. Incidental evidence of workings on East and West Coasts are worth examining to give a flavour of those days, with Nationalisation made inevitable by the Labour victory in the 1945 election.

The records from 1946 show the LNER at least investigating the conduct of its Anglo-Scottish expresses, indicating a desire to return to pre-war standards of running, even if the state of the permanent way was unlikely to permit any major re-accelerations.

In 1946, all three LNER Areas reviewed the running of the 'Flying Scotsman' service, then scheduled to travel between the English and Scottish capitals in the best part of nine hours. The archives show that a dynamometer car was added to the 470-ton rake on two journeys each way over a four-day period in early June. The data obtained appears to have been inconclusive, although presumably intended to test whether any particular sections were too tightly, or too easily, timetabled. An opportunity was also being taken to assess the work of the new A1 Pacific design (technically A1/1, *Great Northern*), but that was in the Southern Area only.

The Scottish managers argued that this was a bad time of year to carry out such testing – they were obviously overruled – and suggested that the up journey was more difficult to operate than the down. This was the opposite of the English operators' conclusion, which was that the down service was harder. Probably, both sides had a good case, but no immediate accelerations took place; indeed the 'Scotsman' was not to better its 1939 timing until 1953.

A more interesting exercise in Anglo-Scottish train timings had been conducted the previous month – more interesting because it involved arranging a special test run. On 21 May 1946, train 361 – a railway officers' special – was run between King's Cross and Waverley on a schedule slightly inside 6.75 hours (399 minutes down, 401 up). The locomotive was A4 No.2512 *Silver Fox* (a rare visitor to Edinburgh), the coach rake comprised six bogies, the passengers were officials exclusively, and the telegraph instructions for signalmen was '4 beats, pause, 4 beats'. This made it clear to all staff that the train was to operate in the style of the pre-war streamliners.

The down run was accomplished punctually, despite the schedule north of Newcastle being only four minutes more than the 'Coronation' timing on this difficult stretch, and despite a speedometer failure at Berwick. Going south the next day, *Silver Fox* did even better, covering the 80 miles between Newcastle and York in 68 minutes and notching up 102mph near Essendine. The official papers concluded from the trial that the track was not yet fully back to pre-war standards – although there must have been easier ways of ascertaining this than doing a 'ton' over it!

These papers from the LNER's Scottish archives – first published by this author in his book *Streamlined Steam* – record exceptional operations. From the same national archive comes a unique and unpublished typewritten record of ordinary timetabled LMS services across the Anglo-Scottish border just after the war, recorded by a private individual paying for his ticket, timing with a stopwatch, and making the same journey every year in his holidays. The recorder was Mr J. Scott, and the train was the 'One o' clock Down', later readopting its 1927-39 title of the *Mid-day Scot*.

Mr Scott's logs comprise four journeys on the midday departure from Euston in 1945, 1946, 1948, and 1949. The journey time and speeds were unremarkable, but the logs are all the more valuable for that – these are typical train runs, timed by a virtually anonymous recorder. (In contrast, if Cecil J. Allen boarded an express train, the driver was often tipped off about his presence, one suspects!). Only the first two journeys should interest us, since Nationalisation came into effect from 1 January 1948, although that year's sample train was headed, not by the usual Stanier Pacific, but by a rebuilt 'Royal Scot' 4-6-0. (It reached Glasgow Central only 1 minute late, this with a load of approximately 420 tons gross from Euston, but on a schedule slower even than 1896.).

The two runs recorded in LMS days involved 'Princess Coronation' Pacifics No.6231 *Duchess of Atholl*, built without streamlining, and the streamlined No.6243 *City of Lancaster* respectively. Both were hauling fifteen bogies, weighing 473 tons tare. Mr Scott estimated the passenger and luggage loads as 52 tons (1945) and 46 (1946). Both locomotives worked through to Glasgow, crews being changed at Carlisle. The slow scheduling reflected the perceived state of the permanent way, and the train, occupying the channel of the crack pre-war 'Coronation Scot', stopped for passenger purposes at Rugby, Crewe and Carlisle. So busy were the trains, that standing times were nearly always exceeded; on both these journeys Crewe Station staff doubled the train's scheduled stand of 3 minutes.

One stop which was made for purposes other than passengers was at Beattock, where banking assistance was taken on both runs, but in 1945 a 'jubilant young soldier' left the train here. One wonders about this – did the young man live at nearby Moffat, and had depended on the train stopping for assistance, to save him changing into a slower train at Carlisle? Or was he confused, or inebriated, and thought he was at Carstairs? We will never know! On this run, Mr Scott had stopped timing by Oxenholme, defeated by fatigue and the falling darkness (this was an October trip). Arrival at Glasgow was 39 minutes late, even on this ponderous schedule.

The 1946 run was undertaken on 22 July, the height of summer. Mr Scott enjoyed this run more, with the *City of Lancaster* – the last Stanier streamliner – reaching Carlisle 4 minutes early. The surplus time was swallowed up by station work, the train departing for the north punctually; arrival in Glasgow was some 6 minutes late, this on a 155-minute schedule for 101 miles.

The modern reader would be astonished at some of the slow speeds recorded on these runs – and deemed unworthy of comment by the recorder. Shap was topped at 18mph on one run, and even the climb to Kilsby, not exactly one of Britain's major summits, was accomplished at exactly 1mph quicker! A speed of 60mph was, of course the official 'maximum', and it appears that even Diesel power was restrained. In 1949, Mr Scott travelled south on a Sunday 'Royal Scot' hauled by the LMS twin Diesels Nos 10000/1, where 60mph was exceeded only twice in the 400-mile journey, which was scheduled to take 45 minutes longer than the weekday timing.

Apart from the operational performance of the 'Coronation' and 'Flying Scotsman' on the East-Coast main line, it has to be said that the running of the Anglo-Scottish trains, whether East or West, was never much more than workmanlike in LMS and LNER days. Failure to bring down journey times before 1932, and the lack of a late-afternoon departure from London to Scotland (and vice-versa) until 1937 – indeed the lack of an early morning service before 1928 – all gave the impression of unimaginative management in an area where imagination was always going to be needed to keep the media interested, and thus encourage long-distance business travelling.

There was of course a third Anglo-Scottish railway route carrying express trains. Indeed, for many years it carried the most sumptuous trains of all, including American-style Pullmans no less, while at the same time offering third-class passenger accommodation on every train – some time before rival lines followed suit. This was the former Midland main line, running north from London (St Pancras) through such major cities as Leicester, Nottingham, Sheffield and Leeds, before addressing the Pennine fells through Settle to Carlisle.

In pre-Grouping days, three expresses left St Pancras in daytime daily for Glasgow, at a time when the West-Coast companies ran only two. All this was very much the hallmark of the Midland Railway, the line which came to dominate so much of the early years of the LMS after 1923.

The Midland reached Carlisle after completing the Settle line in 1876, and there met two allies impatiently awaiting it, the G&SWR and NBR. What is interesting from the viewpoint of post-1923 railway history, is that the Midland was allied to two Scottish companies who were later absorbed by *both* the LMS and LNER.

In 1927, the LMS, then active in naming its most prominent trains, decided to name the two Anglo-Scottish services travelling the former Midland route, as the 'Thames–Clyde' and 'Thames–Forth' expresses, connecting London (St Pancras) with Glasgow (St Enoch) and Edinburgh (Waverley) respectively. The LNER seems to have mounted no objection to this latter naming, although even their lunchtime departure from King's Cross and Waverley (later the 'Heart of Midlothian') bore no name at the time, apart from the unofficial title 'Afternoon Scotsman'. Although slower than the

London–Scotland services from Euston and King's Cross, the two 'Thames' trains served such important English cities as Sheffield, Leeds and Carlisle, as well as Nottingham ('Forth') and Leicester ('Clyde'). Additionally, the pre-war train left Glasgow with through coaches for Bristol (detached at Leeds) and Nottingham (at Trent Junction).

One interesting detail from the pre-war LMS timetable regarding the 'Thames–Clyde Express' was that this was its title only in the down direction; the corresponding up train was timetabled as the 'Clyde–Thames'! Both 'Thames' services began their up and down journeys with their rakes arranged exactly as they were when they left on the previous day's journey. This was because the trains reversed direction at Leeds (City).

The schedules quickened during LMS days, and by 1939 the 'Thames–Clyde' was 17 minutes faster than its 1959 successor while on Scottish metals. Equally, by 1939, the 'Thames–Forth' was covering the Waverley Route 5 minutes faster than was to be the case twenty years later. (The LNER never quite equalled the NBR's 135-minute schedule for the equivalent service in 1901, when at least one driver knocked a further 9 minutes off the schedule north of Carlisle.).

When 'Jubilee' 4-6-0s became available for the Settle and Carlisle line in the mid-1930s, the engine put on at Leeds would work right through to Glasgow on the 'Thames Clyde', but engines were always changed at Carlisle on the Edinburgh service, until 1961, when 'Peak' (Class 44/46) Diesels were assigned to the train.

With Carlisle (Canal) taking delivery of Gresley's A1s and A3s from late in 1928, there must have been a memorable sight at the Citadel station when a harassed-looking ex-Midland Compound brought in the northbound train, to be replaced by a new Pacific half as heavy and powerful again! The late O.S. Nock experienced an exhilarating footplate trip northbound on the 'Waverley' (successor to the 'Thames–Forth') as late as 1957, when he rode a common-user 'Black 5' piloted by a 2P 4-4-0 over Aisgill, although he described himself as 'shattered' on arrival. He then transferred to Canal's A3 No.60095 *Flamingo*, which provided something of a contrast to the 'Wild West' style of railroading he had just undergone.'I can never remember riding on a locomotive in more perfect mechanical condition', he recorded.

Although this was ten years after the demise of the LMS and LNER, this kind of exchange had been going on for nearly thirty years, and one cannot help wondering if the Scottish Area of the LNER was making a point about the superiority of its express locomotive power. Strangely, a Gresley Pacific looked perfectly at home on a rake of LMS carriages – indeed for a short time around 1960, these engines were drafted on the Settle–Carlisle line and headed *both* the 'Thames–Clyde' and 'Waverley' services. Gresley's locomotives featured on two of the three Anglo-Scottish routes during their working careers, and certainly throughout nearly all the period surveyed by this book.

9

Off the Rails

SHIPS, DOCKS, CANALS, BUSES, LIGHTHOUSES, AIRCRAFT, HOTELS, LAUNDRIES, ET CETERA...

As two of the largest commercial concerns in the UK, it was inevitable that the LMS and LNER would diversify into areas other than the 'Permanent Way'. This chapter, therefore, will examine the work of these companies on the water and the air, but also in the world of hotel management. Participation in the running of commercial bus services has already been covered under 'Investment and Economy'.

When it is recalled that no less than two-thirds of the Clyde steamer fleet was railway-owned in 1923, the importance of Scottish railways' maritime operations can be appreciated.

The Caledonian was the largest ship-owning railway company north of the border, although its vessels were operated by a separate Caledonian Steam Packet Co., formed in 1889. At the time of Grouping, the new LMS inherited no fewer than eleven passenger steamers from this 'arm-length' company, one of which was out of commission. The leading 'Caley' steamer was the *Duchess of Argyll*, a 1906 turbine-powered vessel capable of nearly 22 knots, and which had operated on the Stranraer run at one time, as well as on more conventional Clyde duties. She served in both World Wars, during the second conflict as a tender servicing the Atlantic liners disembarking troops at Greenock and Gourock. There were also two dredgers directly owned by the CR, maintaining navigable channels in and out of Grangemouth.

The Glasgow & South Western was no less active on the water than its West-Coast rival, and passed on to the LMS six-passenger steamers, two tugs, and a dredger. Unlike the 'Caley', the G&SWR operated its ships directly, without a 'buffer' in the form of a nominal maritime company. Its steamers were displaying LMS colours by June 1923, although understandably the Caledonian vessels did not begin to exhibit their new ownership until after July. Despite this, the maritime historians, Messrs Duckworth and Langmuir, record that, '... from the beginning of the year, the two fleets were treated as one'. There was no need to incorporate Highland Railway vessels, that company having ceased its maritime activities in the early 1880s.

As already observed, the Northern District of the LMS was able to persuade Euston that it was necessary to create a post of marine superintendent, which was unique to Scotland. After all, the LMS had a presence, through its arm-length company, on Loch Lomond (jointly with the LNER) and, at various times, on Lochs Awe, Etive and Tay. Nor did the LMS commitment to marine matters lessen over the years – five steamers were taken in from the Williamson-Buchanan company in 1935, but the LMS found it convenient to revive the Caledonian Steam Packet Co. for day-to-day operation.

Meanwhile, the LNER's marine responsibilities in the Scottish Area sprang entirely from the enterprise of the former North British Railway in taking to the water (in chronological order), on Forth, Tay, Solway, Clyde, and on Loch Lomond. Six Clyde steamers were inherited from the NBR – which was a direct operator by the time of Grouping – with another two on the Forth, one on Solway, a tug at Dundee and a dredger at Bo'ness. The NBR had run the Granton–Burntisland ferry passage itself, but had leased the Queensferry operation following the opening of the Forth Bridge in 1890. The LNER provided three new Clyde steamers in its twenty-five years of operation – *Jeanie Deans*, *Talisman* II and *Waverley* IV, the last of these now preserved, while losing the *Marmion*, and *Waverley* III to enemy action in the Second World War. As will be seen from the above selection of names, the LNER continued the imaginative North British policy of christening ships (as well as locomotives) with names from the works of Sir Walter Scott, in pleasant contrast to the pedestrian naming policy of LNER vessels on the Humber and operating out of Harwich.

One of the most important ferry services within lowland Scotland was probably the Queensferry passage which the LNER continued for the benefit of road users throughout the company's twenty-five-year life. According to the historian Ian Brodie, it appears that Sir Maurice Denny, from the famous Dumbarton shipbuilding firm, was less than impressed with the rail company's operation of the passage and proposed a modern car ferry service. The LNER showed no interest, but did suggest that, if Denny supplied the vessels, the lease would be his. So in 1934, the Dumbarton company supplied two chain-driven, end-loading ferries, which were to become part of the Forth seascape for thirty years, with a third supplied to BR by Denny in 1949.

But passenger steamers and ferries were not the only vessels flying the new company colours. The former G&SWR tug *Troon* operated out of the Ayrshire harbour of that name, and gave the LMS's new Scottish Local Committee a maritime problem to deal with, barely a fortnight after amalgamation had taken place.

During a storm on 14 January 1923, *Troon* succeeded in putting a crew aboard the distressed Whitby-registered motor schooner *Wyfax*, bringing her safely into Troon Harbour. This counted as salvage – traditionally regarded as a financial bonanza for the salvors – and the matter was placed in the hands of lawyers. The records show that the schooner's owners paid £2,000 to the LMS, plus £25 legal costs. After some deliberation, the rail company decided that £135 of this could be shared among the tug's master and crew – not exactly a generous award, considering that the men had risked their lives to bring this unexpected windfall into the LMS coffers. A later entry in the committee's Minutes that year records the tragic death of the tug's engineer, who drowned in Troon harbour. The company paid £300 to his widow without discussion. The tug itself was sold out of LMS service in 1930, at the same time as its sister, *Ayr*, but was still operating on the Mersey until after the Second World War.

Railway companies were not just content to operate steamer services, but owned a considerable number of dock complexes – indeed, all but the largest docks in Scotland (Leith, Glasgow, Aberdeen, Dundee) were railway-owned.

The LMS inherited docks from all three of its Scottish constituent companies, the largest of these being Grangemouth, where major Caledonian investment resulted in the LMS becoming the owner of quays totalling nearly 3 miles in length (actually, 16,092ft) at this most prosperous of ports. This was the second longest on the entire LMS, being exceeded only by Barrow-in-Furness with its 19,602ft. Second in Scotland was Ayr, with 7,560, while Troon was not far behind on 6,160ft. Other dock installations were owned at Bowling, Fairlie, Gourock, Kentallen (on the Ballachullish branch, and the smallest LMS dock at a mere 64ft), Kyle of Lochalsh, Largs, Oban, Renfrew, South Alloa, Stranraer East and Wemyss Bay.

From the North British, the LNER took over docks at Alloa, Bo'ness, Burntisland, Charlestown (Fife), Fisherrow (Musselburgh), Methil, Port

Carlisle, Silloth and Tayport Harbour. There were also company-owned piers at Craigendoran, Mallaig, North and South Queensferry and Tayport. One of the heaviest of these maritime investments was at the Fife port of Methil, whose location so near to the mouth of the Firth of Forth, and so close to the mines of the Buckhaven area, made it an obvious port for exporting coal. In 1913, the NBR had added considerable investment to that of the Wemyss family here, developing the No.3 dock. In LNER days, there were 25 miles of track within the dock complex, although the coal trade later diminished, along with Fife's great reputation as a leading mining area.

The LNER was represented on a number of public bodies connected with marine matters, but where a railway presence might seem, on the face of it, to be something of a surprise. The company took a seat on the Clyde Navigation and Lighthouses Trusts, the Dundee Harbour Trust, and both the Forth Conservancy board and Forth Pilotage Authority. Curiously, the marine superintendent was not automatically the company's representative on these bodies. In the mid–1940s, although Glasgow-based Capt. Perry was listed on both of the Forth boards, he was omitted from both Clyde bodies in the year 1947. Unless this was a compositional error in the 'Meeting of Directors' publication (i.e. Diaries), it is difficult to see the sense in sending a less-senior staff member – or even worse, a director – to such meetings, although there might have been some kind of members' rotation in operation.

Many of the UK's canals were owned by railway companies before the setting up of a nationalised British Waterways Board, and this may have been a major cause in their decline in the first half of the twentieth century. Tom Rolt, champion of the canals, castigated the indifferent and indeed sometimes hostile attitude of the rail companies – including his own beloved Great Western – towards a rival transport system entrusted to their tender mercies. The canals' capacity for recreation and tourism seems to have gone unnoticed by their uncaring owners, despite ample evidence, even before the Second World War, that the waterways could attract holidaymakers, and thus generate revenue through licensing and mooring charges, in return for little more than maintenance costs.

The longest lowland canal in Scotland is the 38-mile Forth & Clyde Canal, linking Bowling, near Dumbarton, with Grangemouth. At Falkirk it is met by the Union Canal from Edinburgh, and inter-city through journeys were possible from around 1822. However, rivalry from the railways soon demoted passenger traffic to excursion status, and eliminated most of the freight as well, so by 1867 the F & C was taken over by the Caledonian. Thus it was inherited by the LMS in 1923, but the best that can be said of railway ownership of this once-important waterway, was that the canal survived! Although closed to goods traffic in 1962, it is still in a reasonable enough state to provide a recreational function for its owners since 1948, (now British Waterways Scotland). This is more than can be said of the older, 13.25-mile Monkland canal, also taken over by the Caledonian, and then the LMS, but which was lucky to survive until 1952, and much of which was infilled in subsequent years.

One Scottish waterway which did not prosper under LNER control was the Union Canal, connecting Edinburgh with the Falkirk area, and providing an early link between the capital and Glasgow. This fell into the hands of the LNER, having been taken over by the Edinburgh & Glasgow Railway, whose competition it had failed to survive. The North British then inherited it in 1865, and so it passed to the LNER. Within ten years it had ceased to carry freight – specifically road metal from West Lothian to Glasgow, although for some time it had transported horse manure from the capital to country areas for fertiliser. The Union continued intact until 1965, supplying water to Edinburgh's rubber industry, but was closed completely in that year, and was soon culverted in the Wester Hailes area. It has, thankfully, been reopened, and is offering prospects for leisure use.

The LMS and LNER, in their guise as canal owners in Scotland, could at least claim that they did not actually destroy the system altogether. Only one canal closing out of three was probably the best that could be hoped for on a network which was not large enough to sustain an independent existence – the canals never had any direct connection with the English system – and were being managed by transport operators, or at least their successors, which had brought about their impoverishment in the first place.

Both the LMS and LNER invested in what they may have feared was the future of long-distance travel within the UK, by establishing Railway Air Services. This was set up early in 1934, after Sir Eric Geddes, by now the chairman of Imperial Airways, had made approaches to both rail companies with a view to avoiding possible competition. Geddes had already pointed out to his shareholders at an Imperial AGM that the railways had legal powers enabling them to operate air services to foreign capitals as far east as Poland, while he believed that the LMS and LNER would, in turn, fear the introduction of internal British services. He was undoubtedly correct in this latter point; although the technology of air travel was so crude, and aircraft capacity so limited, that the threat from the air was more apparent than real.

In his book on RAS (see Bibliography), John Stroud records that the initial approach from Geddes appears to have been rebuffed by the LNER, but that the LMS was much more receptive, and that Sir Harold Hartley, a vice-president of the LMS, became the first chairman of the new airline. The LNER was nevertheless represented on the board, but it was what might be defined as 'LMS' destinations that were linked by the first major Anglo-Scottish air service – Glasgow, Belfast, Manchester, Liverpool, and London. The first southbound flight took place on 20 August 1934, but headwinds were so strong that the aircraft was grounded at Manchester, and the mail sent on – by train!

The real nature of the transport rival apparently so feared by railway managers – the pre-war passenger aircraft – was best described by Evelyn Waugh in his travel diary, *Labels*. He recounts his experience of flying from London to Paris in 1929, where he disgusted his only fellow-passenger by being sick during the flight and wondering whether it was reasonable to drop his paper bag-full of vomit out of the window! Eventually he decided to put it down the toilet – which amounted to the same as dropping it out of the window – before returning to his wicker seat. A photograph in John Stroud's book on RAS shows passengers bent double with earache after leaving an aircraft in 1945, so it is obvious that rail travel, even third-class rail travel, offered advantages in physical comfort not usually even hinted at!

The transport historian can only look on the rail companies' involvement with Anglo-Scottish air services with some irritation. If the LMS and LNER had competed with each other in their long-distance expresses, with faster average speeds, competitive fares and early-morning and late-afternoon departures, the overall standard of service would have improved, and there might have been even less demand for air services than there was before the Second World War.

Just as the railways' bungled investment in bus services simply empowered the rival bus company, in Scotland anyway, their support for air services betrayed complacency in their response to long-distance passenger requirements. More than this, the railways' support may have given succour to a rival form of transport, itself feeling the winds of recession – no fewer than twelve British-based airlines had failed by 1939.

'We can't improve the service any more than we have', seemed to be the philosophy, at a time when, certainly as the 1930s dawned, each rail company was operating locomotives perfectly capable of cutting 1.5-2 hours from a slothful timetable of no more than three daytime departures daily, on East- and West-Coasts.

By 1939 the LMS held a 40 per cent interest in Scottish Airways, providing services to the Western Isles, and to Orkney and Shetland. The provision of island services was a far more sensible approach to the whole question of whether rail should invest in, and effectively, support, a rival form of transport. The Great Western Railway, for example, was quick to employ this argument in defending its investment in air services to the Channel Islands, even in opposition to its ferry services centred on Weymouth.

Intriguingly, in its 1929 incorporation, SMT, strengthened and refreshed through the generosity of the LMS and LNER, reserved the right to extend its operation to include 'aeroplanes and airships'. Given the dynamic nature of this company, it comes as something of a surprise that SMT Air Services, or similar, did not take to the skies! In fact, around 1932, the company appears to have chartered aircraft to distribute a newspaper with which it was associated, but more might have been expected from this go-ahead organisation.

Railways had owned hotels for decades before 1923, and it is interesting that the smaller Scottish companies were just as active in this area as their larger co-constituents in what became the LMS and LNER. The Highland owned hotels at Achnasheen, Dornoch, Inverness, Kyle and Strathpeffer, the G&SWR at Ayr, Dumfries, Glasgow (St Enoch), and Turnberry, while the GNSR had two hotels in Aberdeen, where the Caledonian and NBR had none. This smaller company also owned the Cruden Bay Hotel, served by its unique narrow-gauge tramway.

The LNER cannot be accused of not trying to promote the attractions of this Aberdeenshire establishment. In 1932, it was possible for a golf enthusiast to travel from King's Cross to and from Cruden Bay for only seven guineas (£7.35), including third-class sleeper London–Aberdeen (on the 'Aberdonian'), full weekend board at the hotel, green fees, and 'hotel car to and from Cruden Bay station'. The advertising material does not divulge if the last specification was actually the tramway – indeed, the text issued in the accompanying leaflet, written by Dell Leigh, reads badly nowadays, with the imaginary English golfer portrayed as 'appalled' at the very idea of travelling to Scotland. Mr Leigh's purple prose was apparently expected to win him over (the potential patron was definitely male).

The North British had owned hotels in Edinburgh and Glasgow, but both that company – and its successor, the LNER – missed an opportunity in not building or acquiring a hotel in the golf capital of St Andrews. (But perhaps not; when a rail-owned hotel was opened there in 1968 it had gone 20 per cent over budget in construction, and made losses for its first three years in a row. Of course, trade might have been better if the railway to the town had not been closed by then!). The NBR also bequeathed eight inns to the LNER, one of them, curiously, in the far-flung rail outpost of Fort Augustus, a destination reached over the leased Invergarry & Fort Augustus Railway after the Highland had given up trying to make anything of this un-remunerative line.

The Caledonian also owned hotels in Scotland's two largest cities, but had at least begun construction of a luxury establishment in the Auchterarder area. Auchterarder was perhaps not deemed commercial enough of a name for the new hotel whose partial construction was taken over by the LMS. This was opened as the Gleneagles Hotel in 1924, and rapidly gained a reputation as the finest golfing hotel in Scotland, if not the world.

However, its gestation period was anything but rapid, the first meeting of the Gleneagles Hotel Ltd taking place as early as October 1913. The meeting venue being the Caledonian's Central Hotel in Glasgow confirmed that company's interest in the venture, which was, theoretically at least, an 'arm-length' company, like the CR's shipping interest. Early proposals for a luxury hotel were costed at £176,000, including the construction of a swimming pool and shooting range, but not including a laundry. It was then decided that the most important of these utilities would be the laundry, so a certain indecisiveness is evident in the archives. Not surprisingly, the Caledonian tightened its control on the enterprise, investing £40,000 in December 1914, half of this as a loan secured by the directors, and all this in lieu of a share prospectus.

The LMS was to inherit a project which, although potentially profitable, was needlessly complicated. 350 acres of land were being purchased from three different estates – always a process fraught with problems for the developer, should one or more of the sellers 'stall' on the sale. Local authority permission also had to be sought for authorisation to build approach roads. It would have been so much simpler to have worked with a single owner, and to have positioned the hotel next to a siding or short branch from an existing railway line in the area. Unsurprisingly, the target opening date of Easter 1915 fell behind schedule – by a mere nine years – and it was left to the LMS to complete this complicated, but worthwhile, project. Caledonian, Highland and North British all owned one-third shares in Perth's Station Hotel.

One enterprise which was literally 'off the rails' but was not strictly pioneered by either the LMS or LNER, was the Bennie Monorail. In April 1930, a local inventor called George Bennie persuaded the LNER to lease him space to erect a monorail system above the former NBR Milngavie branch on north Clydeside. Bennie constructed a substantial cantilevered system with up and down 'running lines'. A propellor-driven coach was suspended under the structure and could reach 50mph even on this short stretch, where it was not possible to test the possibility of a maximum speed of 120mph.

The LNER was probably not the only company keeping a close watch on this development, which is believed to be the first British equivalent of the long-lived monorail system at Wuppertal in Germany, operating since 1901. Presumably, it was the form of propulsion which allowed Bennie and his admirers to claim a first, since the highly successful German system was powered by conventionally conducted electricity. Nothing came of Bennie's initiative – the elevated section was too short to demonstrate any advantage in the propellor system – but the structure was still in place above the Milngavie branch until 1956.

10

Accidents

We have already seen the LNER, during the 1926 General Strike, attempt to defend a civil court case where their inexperienced crew had passed a signal at danger and caused the loss of three lives. The company maintained in court that a declaration of limited – indeed, almost non-existent – liability printed on a ticket, was a sufficient warning to the public that they travelled by train at their own risk. The Court of Session, needless to say, found this defence unconvincing, but it does appear to represent the standard reaction, by the railway companies working in the mid-twentieth century, to any suggestion that they had a burden of care towards their passengers. It is in this light that rail accidents occurring in Scotland between 1923 and 1948 should be assessed by the historian.

The following is a brief, largely chronological, account of fatal accidents on the LMS and LNER in Scotland, but also including those non-fatal incidents which could have been a great deal worse.

The first fatal accident on either company's tracks in Scotland occurred on the LNER at Haymarket on 28 July 1924, when a rear-end collision took place in unseasonably foggy weather. Five passengers were killed in this incident, which Michael Bonavia believed was the result of the lowly status awarded to signalling in the former NBR management hierarchy. The next accident in Scotland was also in Edinburgh, and was bound to happen, as we have seen; it was the collision at St Margaret's on 10 May 1926. Three people lost their lives when the LNER attempted to run a railway service without a full complement of railwaymen.

In the following year, a potentially horrendous accident occurred on the LMS near Stonehaven. A thirteen-coach southbound express was being double-headed (as was frequently the case on the LMS in those days) when a piece of equipment fell from the second locomotive, fouling the coaching stock and causing the leading four coaches to derail. As luck would have it, the train was crossing the Cowie Viaduct, part of whose parapet was carried away by the train's Pullman dining car. L.T.C. Rolt points out, in his classic work *Red for Danger*, that if the couplings had not held fast, the momentum of the rear part of the train would have carried it into the four derailed vehicles, and any or all of them could have fallen into the valley below. The LMS was indeed lucky that no one was killed, and this horrifying incident was not even included in the *Railway Gazette Yearbook*'s annual list of accidents, with its separate listings for passengers and railway staff killed.

A grim year for railway safety throughout the UK was 1928, with particularly bad accidents south of the border, at Darlington and Charfield. In Scotland, two accidents occurred, one on each company's lines. On 12 October, D11 4-4-0 *Colonel Gardiner* failed to climb Cowlairs incline *unbanked*, and slipped back through the smoke-filled tunnel into Queen Street, where a shunting movement was taking place. Four people died, and no fewer than sixty-five were injured. A Queen Street signalman was arrested and tried for culpable homicide.

John Thomas recorded that this prosecution caused great unease among local railwaymen – not least because of the lack of track-circuiting which would have indicated to signalling staff that the D11's train had not cleared the section. There was considerable relief when the driver admitted under oath that his sanders were defective, and that he had reported the matter three times in the previous week. With this confirmed by an inspector, the jury was quick to deliver a 'not guilty' verdict. At least two other accidents of this kind happened at this Glasgow terminus in the age of steam, yet the LNER did not re-equip the layout here with as many safety features as contemporary technology would allow.

Thirteen days later, a night-time accident occurred on the West-Coast main line, which would have surely been prevented by track-circuiting (invented some fifty years earlier). At the wayside signalbox of Wamphray, between Lockerbie and Beattock, the signalman began to pass a slow-moving northbound goods train through his section but, while waiting for it to clear, fell asleep. Two things usually have to go wrong for an accident to happen – not an insurmountable peak for a multi-faceted organisation such as a railway in the 1920s – and by chance the goods train came to a halt in section with a mechanical problem. While the guard checked with the locomotive crew whether he should take detonators back to warn any following trains (and, unfortunately he was none too brisk in doing this)

the signalman was wakened by the box to the south at Dinwoodie, offering him a heavy northbound express. Assuming that the goods had cleared
while he slept, although his signals were still off, he accepted the express,
the newly named 'Royal Highlander'. Four railway staff were killed in the
resulting carnage, and the leading engine, a former Dunalalstair III, went to
the scrapyard. By a miracle, no passengers died.

Scotland's worst accident since Quintinshill occurred at Port Eglinton
Junction, in Glasgow, on 6 September 1934, when there were nine fatal
casualties: six passengers and three staff. This head-on collision took place
on former G&SWR tracks between St Enoch and Paisley, and involved two
local trains each headed by a 2P 4-4-0. The Glasgow-bound train failed to
stop at a junction where the signals were set for the westbound to cross,
and amid the ensuing collision, three of the four footplatemen were killed.
The survivor was the driver who had allegedly passed a signal at danger, and
was arrested and charged with culpable homicide. (Curious that railway
company directors were never arrested for failing to install colour lighting,
track-circuiting, cab-signalling, and so on!).

In his defence, the driver insisted that his clear signal had gone to danger just after his locomotive had passed it, implying indecision on the part
of the signalman, but the Ministry of Transport inspector produced timing
evidence to show that this was impossible. The jury, however, was uncon-
vinced and the wretched driver was acquitted. D.L. Smith, in describing this
incident in his book about the G&SWR in LMS days, refuses to comment
on the cause of the crash, remarking, 'signals can be queer things'.

Two 2P 4-4-0s were also involved in the next LMS accident in Scotland,
one which fortunately, and surprisingly, did not cost any human lives. This
occurred in Galloway in the early hours of 30 December 1935, when the
Down Mail train for Stranraer left the track just after crossing the Loch
Ken Viaduct, both engines and all seven carriages ending up at the foot of
an embankment. Two passengers were slightly injured, but the Royal Mail
sorting tender was damaged beyond repair, and a new vehicle had to be
ordered. The lack of casualties was amazing in the circumstances.

Bad though the Port Eglinton Junction accident was, the Castlecary
accident, of 10 December 1937, was worse. Indeed, with a death-toll of
thirty-five, this was the worst accident in the history of the LNER, with the
second highest death-toll on any of Britain's grouped railways.

Snow was falling on the Glasgow (Queen Street)–Edinburgh (Waverley)
line that December evening, when the Castlecary signalman was informed
that a westbound goods train had been halted by signal at Dullatur, west

of Castlecary, because of points failure farther west. Although he set the Castlecary signals to stop the next westbound train, it appeared to ignore them, and the Dundee–Glasgow train, headed by D29 *Dandie Dinmont*, passed Castlecary at speed, with the frantic signalman waving a red lamp at the engine crew. He then informed Dullatur that the Dundee train was running away 'on right line'. The latter signalman ordered the goods train fireman to put down detonators to protect his train.

Meanwhile, the Castlecary man was asked if he would accept the Edinburgh–Glasgow express, which was running punctually despite the poor weather conditions. One might have expected the signalman to stop the express in view of his belief that there was some kind of problem to the west of him, but he instead had a detailed telephone conversation with the signalman to the east, at Greenhill. The conclusion was that the express could be accepted, and A3 Pacific *Grand Parade* raced westwards at 70mph.

Unfortunately, the train crew from Dundee *had* seen the warning light and had come to a stop. The fireman came back to the box to register his train as stopped, along with the local stationmaster, and they were shocked to find that the Castlecary signalman was prepared to accept another train in section. Rushing from the box, the stationmaster managed to affix one detonator to the track – but it was too late. Although the driver of the express made an emergency brake application, carnage resulted, with casualties in both trains. The resulting death-toll would have been even higher had the modern buckeye couplings not prevented fire breaking out, and the telescoping of the derailed stock. Some passengers at the rear of the train from Edinburgh were even unaware of what had happened farther forward.

In the resulting inquiry, nearly all the blame was attributed to the Castlecary signalman's actions, and his insistence that his distant signal was at danger all the time was refuted by the drivers of both the Dundee and Edinburgh trains. He also claimed that his track circuit indicator was faulty, although it subsequently tested correctly. In retrospect, it appears that the circuiting was advisory only – and could neither prevent duplicated line operation, nor trigger an alarm if the signalman attempted such a manoeuvre. The Ministry of Transport reporter commented on the undesirability of express trains proceeding at full speed in bad weather conditions, and Charles Meacher records that the express driver was reduced to shunting duties, becoming a cleaner after official retirement. For some reason the LNER took a whole year to replace the fireman's overalls, soiled after he had been pinned (unhurt) under coal from the Pacific's tender. But there was also the inconvenient fact that the LNER had *dismantled* a cab-signalling system on the East-Coast main line, which could have been developed and extended in range, and which would have informed the drivers if the distant signal had been at danger, as the Castlecary signalman claimed. So easily could this accident have been avoided, that the LNER decided to use this very main line for the experimental fitting of the Hudd cab-signalling system, one which was operated by electro-magnetism without physical connection between locomotive and track, thus removing the possibility of fouling. Unfortunately, this proved to be a short-lived experiment, with war so imminent, but locomotive expert E.S. Cox was not alone in believing the system worth extending.

Between the Castlecary accident and the outbreak of war some twenty months later, the LMS suffered four accidents on their tracks in the west of Scotland. These included an axle failure on a train at Rutherglen, where two died on 8 April 1938, an employee killed at Wishaw on 4 October of the same year, while there were two accidents in 1939. On 22 February, a collision at Stobcross left one passenger dead, while at Saltcoats on 8 May, two passengers and two staff died after a derailment.

The Highland main line was remarkably free of accidents, but two lives were lost near Aviemore on 5 March 1940 when wagons at the rear of a goods train climbing to Slochd broke away and ran, unimpeded, downhill to collide with 4-4-0 No.14381 *Loch Ericht*, which was waiting to follow and whose crew perished. Following this incident, catch points and sand drags were hurriedly put into place to divert any future runaway, but it is an indication of how accident-free the Highland line had been (particularly in LMS days) that such standard safety features had not been installed previously on this heavily graded line.

Three wartime accidents occurred on the West-Coast main line, one just within Scotland, the other in sight of the Scottish border, in 1940, and one on the former G&SWR line in 1944. In the first, on Guy Fawkes Day 1940, an express and a goods train collided on the diamond junction at Gretna, literally yards from the border. Three people died and no fewer than forty-three were injured. In the second incident, streamlined Pacific *Duchess of Gloucester* derailed at Floriston on 15 May 1940, killing three passengers on a 'Services sleeper'.

In the same year, a signalling defect led to three deaths – all engine crewmen – in Dumfries Station, when on 12 June, a 'Jubilee'-hauled empty stock train was diverted off the main line, smashing into the trailing end of a push-and-pull unit, whose driver had no chance of escape or survival.

Dumfries and Galloway had still one more rail accident to endure before the LMS was nationalised. On 21 July 1945, only weeks before VJ Day, Pacific *Duchess of Atholl*, heading the 1.00 p.m. London-bound from Glasgow (Central), ran through a signal at danger at Ecclefechan, both of her crew dying in the resulting collision. O.S. Nock believed that drifting steam had probably obscured the driver's view, a problem he observed for himself when travelling on the footplate of sister engine *City of Nottingham* on the same stretch of track, not long afterwards. Nock promptly wrote to the company's chief mechanical engineer, H.G. Ivatt, telling him that drivers were having to cut off steam to observe signals and, as a result, smoke deflectors – then affixed only to Polmadie's *Duchess of Montrose* and one other Pacific – were fitted to the entire class.

The LMS did not have a monopoly on wartime accidents, the LNER experiencing a major smash at Cowlairs East Junction in the dusk of 30 January 1942. The 4.00 p.m. express from Edinburgh – some four years after its involvement in the Castlecary accident – ran into a light engine just outside Eastfield engine shed. The Edinburgh driver was killed outright, and there were twelve passenger fatalities, nearly all in the first two coaches. Newspapers reported a noticeable lack of panic among trapped and injured passengers, a fact attributed to the high proportion of service personnel on board, with a female nursing officer organising immediate first aid-procedures. This was the worst Scottish accident in the final decade of both the LMS and LNER.

While the lack of investment in safety devices was one of the most contentious points about the work of these two companies, the sheer volume of traffic carried on their lines is difficult to imagine nowadays, and 99 per cent of passenger and freight journeys were completed without serious incident. This was largely due to the professionalism and dedication of the railway staff, working with the same materials and equipment that had been used in the previous world war.

11

The Second World War

Not only had the First World War imposed undreamt-of traffic burdens on Britain's railway system, but the subsequent demobilisation had two effects. Firstly, there was a completely new attitude to rail travel – hostility. For the first time, large numbers of people – invariably servicemen – had been *forced* to travel long distances by train, whether they wanted to or not, and often in the most uncomfortable of conditions. The historian Hamilton Ellis wrote: 'Many were those who, swaying for hours through the darkness in some crammed long-distance train, vowed that if ever they emerged from this, they would never use a railway again'.

Sailors travelling from Portsmouth to Thurso in a train lacking lavatories were unlikely ever to forget the experience. For many, the train was an instrument of war. They would think twice about taking one to their favourite holiday resort in future years if a bus or coach was available. This was a social legacy that the new 'Grouped' railways were to inherit, and it would not get any better. In fact, more train-bound misery was to arrive in 1939.

A second consequence of the war's end was the proliferation of mechanical skills, particularly in relation to the internal combustion engine. In other words, thousands of men left His Majesty's forces with the skills to run and repair buses, vans, and lorries. It was no longer impracticable to drive, and even own, a bus connecting town and village. The unfettered world of road transport offered almost unlimited opportunities to anyone who wanted to challenge the duopoly of train and tram.

It was in this atmosphere – one growing increasingly inimical to, or at best indifferent to, rail travel, that the LMS and LNER had started their existence. This atmosphere would become even more suffocating when the Second World War began.

The railways' first major passenger challenge, in August and September 1939, was the movement of evacuees. Special trains had to be formed in suburban stations – usually without dock or bay platforms – to transport children, and in many cases their mothers, out of the cities, since a pre-emptive strike by the Luftwaffe was expected by both the Government and the average man and woman in the street. The companies organised no fewer than 500 such trains in Scotland in September 1939, the 322 starting from Glasgow and Clydebank stations carrying the huge total of 123,639 passengers. Even the LNER paddle-steamer *Waverley* (of 1899 vintage) was used to take children away from danger – less than a year later it was sunk rescuing troops at Dunkirk.

Unfortunately, this enforced migration from the cities did not prove to be a 'one-off'. In April 1941, an additional twenty-seven special trains had to be provided, when Clydeside underwent an intensive wave of bombing. It is possible that some of the passengers were being evacuated for the second time; the moves carried out in late summer of 1939 had turned out to be precautionary, perhaps *over*-precautionary, and many a mother and child returned to the city at the earliest opportunity. One official report put the proportion of 'returnees' in Glasgow and Clydebank at no less than 75 per cent by Christmas 1939, and 85 per cent the following Easter. Many of them had to be removed a second time.

There were 31,125 Edinburgh evacuees transported in 129 trains in 1939, many of them heading for such parts of the country as Peeblesshire. One such train was halted in the wilds of that county when gunfire was heard; it turned out to be thunder. Forty-seven trains moved 16,872 people out of Dundee, and the LNER even evacuated 2,187 mothers and children from Rosyth in two trains.

Later in the year, Inverkeithing and the Queensferries (North and South) were added to the list of 'sending' areas, and at least their inhabitants had actually witnessed enemy action at this time. In May 1941, in response to Luftwaffe attacks on the shipbuilding yards, Greenock, Port Glasgow and Dumbarton were also evacuated.

Although railway managers and station staffs worked as best they could to carry out evacuation with a minimum of distress and discomfort for the children, their mothers and teachers, it was inevitable that not all the arrangements would go smoothly. For some reason, the authorities seemed to believe that rural Aberdeenshire was a suitable evacuation area for Glasgow schoolchildren, many of whom had been ordered to report to their schools as early as 7 a.m. on the morning concerned. One teacher complained:

The journey from Glasgow was the most depressing, deplorable and disgust-
ing journey I have ever had the misfortune to make. The train took 12½
hours to reach Aberdeen ... the evacuees were famished when they arrived,
having had no food for 12 hours (most of it had been eaten before leaving
Glasgow). The babies-in-arms kept howling for milk which was unobtain-
able at any station. Mothers began to grow hysterical, two in particular crying
like children.

The above quotation is taken from a report published in 1944 by the
Scottish Council for Research in Education. While listing nightmare journeys such as the above, the publication's editor estimated that 60 per cent of
the transport reports showed that children were 'cheerful' on arrival, with
an additional 25 per cent only 'somewhat depressed'.

The LMS and LNER were dealing with unprecedented logistical
demands, operating to plans drawn up by authorities who had clearly not
taken into account distance from safe areas, and the need for on-route vict-
ualising (as the report called catering facilities). When it is remembered that
everyone in Britain, from the Prime Minister down, believed that air raids
would begin immediately on the declaration of war – perhaps even before,
as George Orwell predicted in a contemporary novel – the strain placed on
railway staff can hardly be overemphasised.

The LMS was warned to have coaching stock ready at no more than
twelve hours notice to clear two ARP (Air Raid Precautions) training
camps at the outbreak of war. Both of these were in markedly remote locations, the English centre at Cark-in-Cartmel in Furness, the Scottish at
Burrow Point just west of Whithorn. The latter was served by the Machars
branch from Newton Stewart, but the logistics of assembling sufficient rolling-stock, moving it along the Dumfries–Stranraer 'Port Road' and then
transporting hundreds of men 'to home stations' – all at short notice – must
have presented a traffic nightmare.

Even as the first evacuation specials were rolling, the authorities were
re-imposing the same level of government control on the railway companies which had only been lifted eighteen years earlier. On 1 September
1939, the Minister of Transport announced the taking over of the railways,
and the establishment of a Railway Executive Committee, headed by the
LNER's Sir Ralph Wedgwood. This communicated directly with the operating departments of the 'Big Four'.

At least the companies were able to approach their new wartime tasks
realistically, with passenger stock being freed up for troop and evacuation

specials by reducing regular services, although this meant a major loss in normal passenger revenue. At Glasgow (St Enoch), for example, the number of originating passenger journeys dropped from 18,530 in August 1939 to a mere 5,401 in the following October, with gross revenue, including parcels and a diminishing number of season tickets sales, generating only £11,839 in the latter month, compared to £31,699 in the previous August.

No attempt was made to continue prestigious express services; the 'Coronation' and 'Coronation Scot' ceased running even before Chamberlain had made his gloomy announcement of war on 3 September 1939. Restaurant cars were rapidly withdrawn – perhaps too rapidly – before on-platform catering facilities could be established for troop trains, and some were reintroduced in the following month. (The new requirement for all passenger carriages to be unlighted – until appropriate lightshades could be fitted – meant that it was too dangerous for kitchen car staff to cater while on the move in a darkened train anyway.). There were further restaurant car withdrawals in 1942, with a complete ban on on-board catering in the run-up to D-Day in 1944. Travelling post offices continued until October 1940 – they were allowed lighting – but all lineside exchange facilities were withdrawn at the outbreak of war.

Such services as the 'Flying Scotsman', far from being non-stop, were scheduled to stop some four times per journey, for example, at Berwick-on-Tweed. The LMS retimed its Anglo-Scottish passenger trains to take an average of just over ten hours between London and Glasgow.

Another variety of traffic anticipated by the planners in the early days of war was ships' ballast. This consisted of colliery waste to be transported (end-door wagons were specified) to nearby ports, although only Liverpool and Birkenhead were mentioned in 1939 documents.

All this was a practical concession to reality, and a welcome change from the conduct of pre-Grouping companies in 1914, when a 'business-as-usual' policy not only interfered with the companies' ability to devote staff and rolling-stock to the demands of war, but caused great offence (as Siegfried Sassoon recorded) to soldiers and sailors home on leave, or because of wounding, greeted with the sight of civilians eating more than their fill in station restaurants, or indeed in restaurant cars.

Just before the outbreak of war, the LMS issued a pamphlet instructing staff of their new working procedures. Company offices were to be specially protected at Carlisle, Edinburgh, Kilmarnock, Motherwell, Polmadie and St Rollox, although the degree of fortification, if any, was unspecified, and only Euston was to be provided with office accommodation underground. LMS offices at Aberdeen, Inverness and Perth had to make do with sandbags, although one suspects that was the case with the large Scottish offices too. Sand was a plentiful commodity early in the war, important in fire-fighting as well as for filling sandbags. No less than 8,500 tons were stored at five LMS sites in Glasgow, including Buchanan Street and St Enoch termini, but not, curiously, at Central. Crew Junction in Edinburgh stored 1,500 tons.

On the LNER, the north side of the Waverley station, the abandoned tunnel from Canal Street (by then part of the Waverley, now opposite platform 19) down to Scotland Street was converted into emergency accommodation for Control staff for both Edinburgh District and also Scottish Central District. It appears to have been seldom, if ever, used.

With six months of the war to go, by the end of 1944, the LMS alone had operated an extra 80,000 special trains at the request of the armed services. Speaking of services in the Far North in March 1940, the LMS president, Lord Stamp (who tragically perished in a bombing raid the following year) pointed out that, although there had been complaints about such lines being 'carried by the rest of the system… I leave you to put a value on those lines in wartime'. He specified that parts of the former Highland system were seeing a 40 per cent increase in traffic. Unfortunately, civilian passengers were deprived; the Strathpeffer branch service was reduced to one passenger train per week! Small wonder that closure followed the next year, when local hotels returned to catering for a civilian clientele.

While the subsequent level of war-related traffic and reduced manpower and maintenance was to virtually bring the railways to their knees, there were some direct benefits from government control, for example the construction of 'occupation loops' on main lines which should have had them years before. Five were installed on the Highland main line between Perth and Inverness alone in 1942. (Interestingly, Michael Harris has pointed out that the fastest-ever northbound timing between Perth and Inverness was timetabled at this time.). Loops were also installed on the East-Coast main line north of Berwick in the Reston area. New locomotives such as Stanier 2-8-0s, and 'Austerity' 2-8-0s and 2-10-0s, and 0-6-0 saddle tanks, were leased to the home railways before being shipped overseas. US-built 'Bolero' 2-8-0s were shipped into the UK, and over 200 of them were used on the LMS and LNER while awaiting the opening of the 'Second Front', but the companies were still probably the long-term losers.

The Firth of Forth was the first part of the UK to experience enemy air activity. Although captured Luftwaffe maps highlighted the Forth Bridge, and the earliest aerial dogfights of the war took place over the Forth and the Lothians, with a naval cruiser being bombed (without incident) a few cables' length from the bridge, no harm came to the structure in six years of war.

Curiously, the FBR board (see the chapter on Joint LMS/LNER operations) seemed fairly relaxed about any enemy threat to their centrepiece. The records show, in fact, that the directors were more concerned about the safety of a silver model of the bridge in the possession of the Science Museum at South Kensington. On hearing that the museum was unable to insure the model, the FBR directors promptly did so themselves, their policy being worth £700. Otherwise, there is little in the company records about war precautions, other than a request from the Admiralty for fittings for an anti-submarine boom to be attached to the bridge piers, something the FBR insisted on doing with their own staff and billing the Navy.

While the FBR directors (including six LNER members) may have been fairly casual about the wellbeing of their bridge, the official LNER war history tells a slightly different story. It seems that, at least early in the war, no train was allowed to cross with passengers keeping hand luggage in their possession – all such personal effects had to be stowed in the guard's van. Presumably, this was on the assumption that a saboteur might throw a grenade-sized bomb out of the window, although what damage this would do is debateable, considering the over-engineered nature of the Forth Bridge.

Another safety feature was the deployment of sentries at each end of the structure, based at a camp at Dalmeny. The alarm was sounded one evening when a flaming object was thrown into the camp from a southbound passenger train which had just crossed the Forth. After the burning projectile had been extinguished, the police were called and were waiting to interview passengers on their arrival in Glasgow. The culprit appears to have been a cinema courier who had noticed that a can of film – probably of the silver nitrate variety – had combusted during transit so he promptly threw it out of the window. But why wasn't it in the guard's van? The official history fails to resolve this contradictory information!

As if the privations of total war were not enough, the 1940s were particularly noted for their severe winters and glorious summers. The railways had to endure exceptionally bad weather in that first winter, particularly at the end of January 1940. Six miles of the LNER's West Highland line were blocked by 10ft of snow for no less than a fortnight, and a double-headed snowplough marooned. The LMS lines to Stranraer were similarly affected, with 15ft of snow at the Swan's Neck. Stranraer had to have yeast for bread-making flown in from Northern Ireland. Even the Glasgow

(St Enoch)–Carlisle main line was blocked by four locomotives stuck at New Cumnock.

The Highland section of the LMS experienced severe weather in January 1942, when two trains northbound from Inverness to Wick were stranded at the intermediate stations of Kinbrace and Forsinard. Steam heating was maintained until the locomotives' water supplies gave out, but the RAF was required to drop food supplies as the snow siege lasted into a fourth day. It is an indication of the continuing problem posed by weather in that decade, that, when a journalist managed to interview one of the train guards, the latter pointed that this kind of thing had happened to him no fewer than three times in the previous winter! On this occasion in 1942, so strong were the winds, that one passenger was convinced that the buffeting of the carriages in the dark was a sign that the train was under way and would soon reach Wick!

The west of Scotland, which had escaped bombing in the First World War, more than made up for this in the Second World War, with Clydebank and Greenock suffering in particular. The LNER official history fails to mention the former shipbuilding town, although reconstruction plans drawn up in 1945 budgeted for the rebuilding of three local stations in the area. The LMS regarded Greenock as one of its most severely bombed locations anywhere in the UK; even when not being targeted, Greenock featured as a transatlantic port, in particular being heavily used to disembark US forces ferried over on such liners as the Cunard 'Queens' – built on this very river. (Tendering duties were undertaken by, among others, the *Duchess of Argyll*, the former Caledonian, and now the LMS, turbine steamer in its second tour of wartime service.).

Glasgow, as already noted, underwent two waves of civilian evacuation, the bulk of which was handled by the LMS, but transporting civilians was the least of the company's worries. Even two years before the end of the war, the number of service personnel processed through the LMS Glasgow District was over 3 million since 1939.

In Edinburgh, a fire at the LMS goods station at Lothian Road illuminated the night sky in November 1939, providing a homing beacon for the Luftwaffe before it could be extinguished. Fourteen wagons were burnt out with no less than 270 tons of chocolate being destroyed. Fortunately there were no bombers around to take advantage of the disarray.

One LMS employee in Scotland decorated for gallantry was John Quinn, a ganger employed in the Coatbridge area. When a member of a permanent-way crew standing back to allow the passage of a train, Mr Quinn saw that one of his colleagues, a woman ganger, had stepped too far backwards, and had fallen under the wheels of a coal train which was slowly picking up speed. Although the unfortunate woman was already injured, she attempted to crawl out from under the moving wheels. With no regard for his own safety, Mr Quinn threw himself under the train and held the woman down until it was safe for her to be extricated. Although he undoubtedly saved her life, she still lost both feet.

There was heroism on the East Coast, too. On 11 November 1941, the footplate crew of the down 'Flying Scotsman' misidentified enemy planes as friendly, and proceeded north from Berwick Station past Marshall Meadows, and towards the Scottish border at Lamberton. The train was then strafed from end to end, with Fireman Hay of Gateshead being unfortunately shot through his arm from elbow to wrist. The bullet popped out of his hand on to the footplate, but even more remarkably, Mr Hay carried on firing all the way to Edinburgh, where common sense prevailed, and he was driven straight to the Royal Infirmary. Normally, all trains stopped at the nearest signalbox during an air raid; a locomotive boiler was a favourite target for trigger-happy air crews. On one occasion, all East-Coast traffic was halted because of a raid on Liverpool, far to the west.

The borders region was not expected to be in the forefront of enemy action, leading to its use as an evacuation area. But even this rural part of Scotland could pose logistical problems for the rail companies. For example, the town of Galashiels was chosen as the Scottish centre for the storage and distribution of gas-masks. In the year leading up to war, no less than 2,500 tons of masks were moved into, and then out of, Galashiels by rail. Another unexpected logistical challenge originated from a decision, fairly late in the war, that all available straw from East Anglia should be sent to South Leith, for use in Midlothian paper mills. According to the official LNER historian, this traffic, 'drove all three Areas of the LNER nearly frantic ... I still found bitter memories of this straw, one year after the end of the war'.

One administrative misjudgment concerned the disposal of engine ash from Edinburgh loco depots, with LNER Scottish chief George Mills (successor to Jim Calder, 1934–41) identifying an unnamed moorland sid-ing (perhaps Borthwick, though long-established) where the offending ash could be dumped. Rather tactlessly, Mills informed local residents that the dumping might have the supplementary benefit of acting as a decoy fire to attract enemy bombers away from city targets. Not surprisingly, local people liked this proposal less the more they heard about it and, according to the official history, Mills found himself threatened with arrest by the chief constable if he went ahead with the dumping during the period of blackout.

Blackout conditions – designed to deny enemy bombers any navigational assistance – were a trial for citizens and railways alike. In darkened stations, platform edges were whitewashed, a practice continued after the war, but all extemporised solutions to working in near darkness could barely compensate for normal conditions. Shunting staff were particularly at risk working in unlit yards, with their hand lamps stuffed with paper to reduce the beam. Footplate staff had to swelter under tarpaulins designed to prevent shafts of firelight escaping; these must have been purgatory on warm summer nights. Norman McKillop claimed that the blackout made signal sighting easier in the dark, but his was a lone voice; every other reference to blackout conditions in railway operation emphasises the dangers involved.

Even in the signalbox, conditions were infinitely worse than in peacetime. In the two power boxes at Edinburgh (Waverley), yellow lighting was installed, with the windows being painted transparent blue. The official history does not record how successful this novel colour scheme was, but it appears that yellow light created unacceptable eye-strain.

All railway resources were bound up with the war effort –from engineering plants to fashionable hotels. Cowlairs works, which the LNER had downgraded to a repairs-only status in 1924, was identified by the Government as a potential weapons factory a year before war was declared, and was the first in the UK to turn to munitions production. It was soon making aircraft wings for forwarding to a commercial plane-maker at Dumbarton, but widened its output to include tank turrets, gun mountings, Inglis bridges and miscellaneous, but doubtless vital, forges and stampings, most of which were supplied to Gorton (the former GCR works in Manchester). US-built 'Bolero' locomotives were modified at Cowlairs (they arrived without handbrakes) before being let loose on UK metals while awaiting Operation 'Overlord' in June 1944. (One managed to become derailed while passing through Edinburgh's Princes Street Gardens.).

Two-thirds of the Cowlairs workforce was made up of women, and this was the first British works to train and employ women riveters. Unfortunately, it has to be said that this dilution of the regular workforce appears to have compromised the reputation that Cowlairs had previously enjoyed for its craftsmanship. Geoffrey Lund, while wartime shedmaster at Haymarket, felt that the works staff was incapable of keeping Gresley's P2 Class in proper working order, particularly in handling problems which developed with the super-heaters and smokebox saddles. Significantly, the Scottish Area usually

sent its Pacifics to Doncaster or Darlington for overhaul, except immediately after their introduction in 1924.

A lesser sacrifice for both LMS and LNER was the loss of hotel revenue.
The luxury LMS establishment at Gleneagles became a military hospital,
as did the company's hotels at Turnberry and Strathpeffer, with Glasgow
Central's hotel undertaking a partial military role. The last-named appears
in literature, as the locus of a crucial scene in Evelyn Waugh's classic wartime
trilogy *Sword of Honour*, where the nation's officer class is finally brought
down to the level of what Waugh viewed as the despised 'Common Man'.

The LNER lost the Aberdeen Palace Hotel, destroyed by fire in October
1941 with, unfortunately, the loss of six lives. Meanwhile, the Cruden Bay
Hotel was taken over by the army, becoming a barracks for the Gordon
Highlanders. Its laundry had taken in the washing for all Divisional establishments, ferried from the Boddam branch railhead to the hotel laundry
over 930 yards of the unique 3ft 6.5in (1,070mm)-electric tramway. But
Cruden Bay's brush with the military was too much for it. The tramway
closed at the end of 1940, and the hotel failed to recover with the arrival of
peace, being demolished in 1947. The loss of this, once the GNSR's flagship,
was an un-noticed victim of the Second World War.

As already mentioned, the LNER lost the former NBR paddle-steamer
Waverley to enemy bombing when evacuating troops from Dunkirk. A
second loss was the *Marmion*, also inherited from the North British, but
sunk by the Luftwaffe at Harwich in 1941. Meanwhile, the *Jeanie Deans* and
the *Talisman* survived the war in military service, the latter renamed HMS
Aristocrat, while a reduced Clyde service was maintained by the LNER
using the 1888-built *Lucy Ashton*, which missed only one day's service in six
and a half years before peace returned. The LNER's reconstruction plans,
drawn up in 1945, and budgeting for a new paddle-steamer, commented
that the doughty *Lucy Ashton* was now in its fifty-sixth year.

At Burntisland and Methil, where the LNER owned the docks, new
tracks were laid to the end of one of the harbour walls, and on these were
marshalled redundant wagons piled with scrap iron. In the event of inva-
sion, these were to be pushed over the edge in order to block the harbour
from becoming a landfall for the Wehrmacht. The authorities could not be
faulted for their determination to thwart the enemy, but one wonders just
how high the capture of Burntisland and Methil ranked in Germany's war
aims!

There should be no doubt in the reader's mind about the effects of the
Second World War on the nation's railway system. The four main railways

emerged from the twentieth century's second major conflagration with only 70 per cent of their targets achieved on track maintenance – perhaps not so shocking nowadays, but unprecedented in the mid-twentieth century. One passenger carriage in eight was under, or awaiting, repair in 1946, while the percentage of locomotives out of service had gone up by a third since 1938, and now stood at one in twelve. Goods wagons under or needing repair had increased by no less than 281 per cent since 1938! One economist (Denys Mumby) summed it up in bloodless academic terms, by describing this as, 'net disinvestment on the railways for many years on a massive scale'. When in 1946, the Chancellor of the Exchequer, Hugh Dalton, stated that, 'the railways are in very poor physical shape', no one argued.

Yet the railways had been controlled by Government since 1939, and had played a vital part in the Allied victory, performing every task asked of them, often with rail staff laying down their lives to ensure that the trains kept moving. While the coming Nationalisation was perhaps not everyone's answer to the need for transport modernisation, there seems to be a strong case, moral as well as economic, for a programme of major investment. It was not to be.

12

Towards Nationalisation

Not surprisingly, all the four Grouped companies campaigned against the prospect of Nationalisation, with the LNER and LMS very much at the forefront of the protest at the end of the Second World War. In 1946, the LNER announced a development programme, entitled 'Forward' (the company's motto centred in the rarely seen coat-of-arms), promising the 'restoration of prewar standards of service', and suggesting that only the need for track improvements was delaying the return of the flagship stream-liners. The ordering of a new paddle-steamer for the Clyde (the *Waverley*) was one positive note, but, more prosaically, the announcement of a lick of paint for 300 stations was not inclined to inspire confidence.

The LMS campaign included the publication of a pamphlet called *A record of a large-scale organisation*, with the reader left in no doubt as to which organisation was intended! The compiler emphasised the sheer scale of the company, still the biggest in the UK at the time. Certainly, a railway with nearly 300,000 wagons and staff of a quarter of a million was an industrial force to be reckoned with, but perhaps more impressive was the claim that passenger train miles had gone up from 7,600 million in 1923 to 13,400 million in 1945, despite the retraction in the number of route-miles (not specified). Less impressively, it appears that, even after nearly a quarter of a century, barely 51 per cent of the locomotive stock was built post-Grouping, and even that must have included pre-1923 designs, which continued building after that year, the Midland 'Compounds' being an obvious example.

In the same year, the LMS produced a question-and-answer booklet, which was perhaps less than fully convincing about the joys of private ownership. When answering the question, 'Why no seat reservations?', the company quoted a lack of staff to undertake this task. The statement that no fewer than 14,213 company employees were still drafted in HM Forces, and that 1,600 passenger vehicles had been lost or scrapped during the war, may have left the reader wondering if, in fact, public ownership might very well be a good idea after all! The company's stated aim that 'The LMS exists to serve the public' was only partly true, since it also had to serve its shareholders, an obligation that Nationalisation was about to remove.

So much for the public posturing. What the LNER was hoping to do in the way of reconstruction – very much a 'buzz word' in the 1940s – is best revealed in an internal 1945 document preserved in the National Archives of Scotland. It is worth examining this document in some detail (see Bibliography) as it illustrates what the company's own senior staff perceived as the LNER's operational shortcomings.

Internally at least, the company addressed the question of how and where to direct its future investment in the 'Post War Reconstruction Programme', produced in July 1945 with a detailed Area-by-Area survey of the company's future operational needs. In the two copies examined by this author, the Scottish Area section is the only one of the three which is printed; the other two are typed. It was as if the Scots had been quietly preparing themselves for this! Having said that, the 'bill' for Scottish reconstruction only came in at £4,042,828 as compared to £6,140,000 for the North Eastern Area, and £10,556,500 for the Southern, although in the case of the last-named case this may have included responding to bomb damage. These costings were all listed for 'first priority' requirements, curiously, as mentioned earlier, a mere 'second priority' was the installation of colour-light signalling on the East-Coast main line north of Marshall Meadows (Berwick-on-Tweed). Electrification rated a zero in the costings column for all Areas, and there were no entries under 'shipping' for any Area except Scottish.

The 'Programme' is basically a 'wish list', and its compilers must have realised that theirs was something of an academic exercise as they read the election results coming in around that time. Trumpeting an ambitious Nationalisation programme, a new Labour government enjoyed a huge parliamentary majority following the July 1945 general election and, to its credit, lost no time in carrying out its election promises, a declaration on rail Nationalisation following on 19 November 1945. Nevertheless, this was still in the future when the Scottish LNER planners first began to make their contribution to the company reconstruction agenda, and it is interesting that the largest-scale projected improvements in Scotland were to be in freight facilities and motive power depots.

As if to confirm the lack of pre-war investment in goods services by the LNER in Scotland, the 1945 programme called for a marshalling yard to be built at Alloa at a cost of £141,000, and no less than £2¼ million to be spent on a new yard at Portobello, although, confusingly, that was listed as only a 'second priority'. Cadder yard, the LNER's biggest in or near Glasgow, was to receive two improvements. The yard staff, who numbered no less than 128, with a maximum of 56 on duty at any one time, were to enjoy new catering and restroom facilities, although the new buildings, costed at £11,000, would have been split between the opposite ends of the 0.5-mile-long yard. Meanwhile, an additional £7,000 would be made available to improve the water supply, and what the footplate crews were having to put up with at the time is an eye-opener.

Water was apparently taken from the Kirkintilloch Main (this was of course when local authorities controlled water supply) at a rate of 30,000 gallons a day. The only snag was that shunting locomotives, and visiting train engines, required 70,000 a day. The LNER was prepared to budget £7,000 to fit up its own supply from a standing source in order to provide its staff with this essential tool. Needless to say, the crew of any steam locomotive which 'ran dry' and caused the fusible plugs to melt, faced a disciplinary charge.

One of the few passenger stations set to benefit, if the LNER had been allowed to continue, was Glasgow's Queen Street, although the principal expenditure was to be on the operational side, with the installation of colour-lights and track-circuiting (at an estimated cost of £115,200). But that was not going to happen in the days of private enterprise.

Motive power depots were also to be improved, and not before time. Hawick was to have its shed removed from its position in what was practically the middle of the goods yard, and moved to the location of the existing turntable near the North signalbox. This much-needed improvement was costed at £107,731, and was never to take place, the locomotives of what became 64G in BR's time, remaining within a stone's-throw of the down station platform until rendered redundant by Dieselisation, and later, complete closure.

Both Edinburgh's Haymarket and Glasgow's Eastfield were to enjoy various technical improvements – despite the fact that they were far from being the oldest or most constricted depots. The former had fourteen locomotives awaiting repair at the time of publication – listed very exactly as 17.72 per cent of its complement, while the water supply was so poor that it was taking twenty minutes to fill a Pacific's tender. The plan promised action to reduce this time to five minutes. Meanwhile, Eastfield was credited with catering for a 62 per cent increase in 'high capacity' engines, i.e. those over 25,000 pounds tractive effort. More to the point, neither was as cramped as St Margaret's or Parkhead, both of which were more deserving of investment.

At Aberdeen's Kittybrewster, the depot's 65ft-diameter turntable was described as 'virtually worn out'. Its replacement by a 70ft-table was costed at £10,646, but that sum would include a new sand drier for the depot, as well as a new oil tank and taller water columns. Curiously, the LNER General Appendix to the Working timetables issued in 1947, lists the depot turntable at 60ft; whichever figure was accurate, this indicates that the 70ft-table requested had not materialised. Other former GNSR depots to be improved included Keith, Elgin, Maud, Peterhead, Craigellachie, Fraserburgh and Ballater. The first two were to receive 70ft-turntables, the remaining five, 60ft-tables – long enough to accommodate the new B1 4-6-0, 'which type engine', the document records, 'will be most useful in the Great North of Scotland section [the Northern Division of the LNER's Scottish Area] and will avoid a considerable amount of double-heading with consequent savings in manpower and fuel'.

These 'improvements' were in fact a fairly basic listing of essential depot facilities, and betray the lack of investment in locomotive support services in the years prior to the war. Interestingly, when the new BR regional controller, T.F. Cameron, wrote a morale-boosting article for the nationalised body's magazine, he listed some of the improvements put in place by the LNER. The rebuilding of Thornton engine-shed was the only specific achievement in Scotland that he mentioned.

Non-operational buildings set to benefit, if Nationalisation had not intervened, were the company HQ at 23 Waterloo Place, Edinburgh, for which £500,000 was budgeted for a rebuilding job, or for purchasing a new site altogether. It was proposed to move the District office from Burntisland to Kirkcaldy, but there were to be only minor changes at Glasgow – home to the goods manager and marine superintendent – and Aberdeen. Even the Joppa laundry in Edinburgh, less than twenty years old, was to be modernised and re-equipped to increase capacity and allow the closure of Cruden Bay.

Meanwhile, as noted earlier, a new *Waverley* paddle-steamer was proposed, and happily, this was to become a reality. The LNER's last marine representative is still with us, and is a familiar sight up and down the UK's coastline. £100,000 was allocated in 1945 for its construction, specifically to replace the fifty-six-year-old *Lucy Ashton*, with enough left over to allow modernisation of the *Jeanie Deans* and *Talisman*.

Two years after this reconstruction document was compiled, the LNER indulged in another flight of fancy which can only baffle the historian, and doubtless puzzled senior staff at the time. This was a plan, prepared in some detail, and approved by the LNER board on 24 July 1947, to introduce twenty-five Diesel-electric locomotives on to Anglo-Scottish passenger services. With each unit generating 1,600hp, but intended to be used in pairs, it is not hard to perceive the company's determination to match the LMS's introduction of units 100000/1, which would have almost exactly the same power-rating, and were planned to enter service by the end of the year.

What is particularly interesting to the Scottish reader was the plan's iden- tification of Edinburgh as a major servicing point, in contrast to the LMS which ran its Diesels into Glasgow on a 'there-and-back' basis. No less than £200,000 of a projected £260,000 was to be spent in the Scottish capital on depot facilities. This was because property values in London were seen as a major obstacle to finding a new site for housing and repairing Diesels, while the through configuration of Waverley and the comparative abun- dance of 'skilled staff' in Edinburgh were additional advantages. There was something of an implied compliment to Haymarket depot in all this, but the proposed major depot was not to be there, but on the other side of the city. Leith Central was proposed as a suitable servicing centre; the fact that it was a passenger station, plumb in the middle of its community, was not mentioned in the document!

The plan was quite detailed, but was never likely to come to fruition as the LNER approached its end on 31 December. Curiously, in 1947, the LNER was in the process of introducing no fewer than eighty-two Class A1 and A2 Pacifics to the company's lines, and that figure does not include those locomotives converted to 4-6-2 classification from the P2 Class. Additionally, the plan to convert to oil-fuelled traction, so soon after a war when this commodity had to be imported at so much expense in shipping and crewmen's lives, seems puzzling. Admittedly, fuelling of steam engines by oil was also very much in favour in 1947, but a steam locomotive can always be converted back to coal fuel in the event of a national emergency. Within ten years, such a restriction on fuel imports did in fact take place with the closure of the Suez Canal, and early Diesel introductions – not least the Edinburgh (Waverley)–Glasgow (Queen St) service in 1957 – had to be implemented gradually.

Just as the 1923 Grouping of Britain's railways was the product of a polit-ical decision, so Nationalisation was a development imposed from above. The incoming Labour Government in 1945 had such a massive major-ity that no one involved in politics expected anything except a full-scale Nationalisation programme. When the four main railways became British Railways on 1 January 1948, the *Railway Magazine* lamented the lack of debate about the appropriateness of the measure, but with a Labour major-ity of 146 at Westminster, politicians and transport managers simply accepted their fate. It was left to such inspired amateurs as Tom Rolt to keep the flag of private enterprise flying in the world of British railways – even if it meant reviving a Welsh slate line initially – and Scotland's railways had no part to play in that field of endeavour.

Evidence that the British class system was alive and well – or at least the political perspectives associated with social distinction – can be gathered from reading the final issues of the LMS and LNER magazines, as well as the new periodical which followed it. In the last issue of the LNER organ, chairman Sir Ronald Matthews thanked the company's staff for their work over the years, and concluded with a morale-boosting message: 'the railways have never failed the country and they will not fail it now'. He viewed the railway system as entering into another time of trial, almost as if fighting a continuation of the Second World War. His staff, meanwhile, greeted that New Year with parties!

The fact that the magazine in which Matthews was writing had only 23,000 subscribers – barely one LNER staff member in ten – indicates that the editorial line was a little out of sync with that of the workforce.

Meanwhile, David L. Smith, best remembered nowadays as the historian of the old G&SWR, had been campaigning for a reduction in Scottish rail fares, particularly in rural areas. As the life of the LMS neared its end, he compared bus and rail revenues in south-west Scotland, but failed, perhaps, to take into account that comparative fare rates were often rendered irrel-evant by stations being situated some way from the villages or towns they supposedly served. Gatehouse of Fleet Station was seven miles from the town of that name, for example! In the circumstances, no aspiring passenger could be blamed for turning to a bus service which might very well run past their door.

Mr Smith went to the trouble of organising a petition calling for rail fares to be more competitive with road, but found LMS officials unyield-ing in their counterargument – that previous fare reductions had increased losses, not profits. Mr Smith responded that the reductions had not gone far enough. A return fare from Ayr to Glasgow by train, he pointed out, cost 8*s* 2*d* by train, but only 4*s* 6*d* by bus. But, he concluded, 'Scottish officials were not wholly to blame, Euston sat immovable'.

Curiously, Mr Smith might well have been impressed by the flexible, and admittedly often confusing, fares structure of the present day, where long-distance rail tariffs can often rival even the bus. Nevertheless, the late Mr Smith's argument for *cheaper* fares for the Scots was a striking contrast to the boardroom view of 1923, that fares and freight rates in Scotland would have to be *higher* in order to establish a viable working base. Who was right – the directors, or the professional railwayman who lived and breathed railways night and day during those twenty-five years of Scotland's 'Big Two'? History cannot tell us now.

Perhaps Mr Smith can be allowed the final comment on the contribution of London's railways to Scottish life between 1923 and 1948. He was writing about the LMS alone, but his comments could apply equally to the LNER:

> Twenty-five years of the LMS – it was not a long life for a railway, but it had been an eventful one. I marvelled at the wealth of incident, the good work, the brave endeavour… Forget the final tragic decline, it only highlighted the happy times of pre-war and wartime LMS.

Bibliography and Sources

COMPANY RECORDS

These have been used as the basis for the material in this book whenever possible. The originals can be viewed at the National Archives of Scotland (NAS) in Charlotte Square, Edinburgh. A company index is bound in the first volume of 'British Railway Records' and it should be checked first to ascertain the placing of the material in the collection. For example, the LMS/LNER files on 'Areas of Joint Interest' are filed before either of these companies' papers. (Also note the imprecise alphabetisation of the index – e.g. 'Lanarkshire' filed before 'Labour' etc – but being in page form, it is easily scanned through).

In addition to company papers dealing with board matters, the following files have afforded primary information on the miscellaneous subjects indicated:

BR/LNE/8/782 (1924 LMS/LNER cartel arrangements)
BR/LCA(S)/177, BR/LMS/4/281, BR/LNE/8/779 (General Strike)
BR/LMS/26/108 (LMS/LNER investment in SMT)
BR/LNE/8/328 (1933 review of Express Train services)
BR/LNE/8/340, BR/LNE/8/387 (High speed trials)
BR/LNE/8/359 (Log of the 'Coronation')
BR/LNE/4/452 (1945 Reconstruction programme)
BR/RSR/4/173 (Glasgow St Enoch passenger register)
BR/RSR/5/261 & /262 ('The One o'clock Down').
GD/360/53 & /85 (LMS and LNER Directors' diaries [various titles])

Needless to say, the author acknowledges with thanks the helpfulness and prompt service provided by the excellent staff of the NAS. The omission of these railway records from the otherwise authoritative *Bibliography of British Railway History*, whose most recent supplementary volume is published by the National Railway Museum at York, is a continuing disappointment.

Assistance is also acknowledged from the staff of the National Library of Scotland, and the public libraries of Edinburgh, Carlisle, Dumfries and South Ayrshire (particularly Sheena

Andrew).The Royal Commission on Ancient and Historical Monuments, and Royal Institute of Architects in Scotland, were both extremely helpful in assisting with station research.

Individuals who have assisted include Geoff Hughes (particularly for supplying unpublished material concerning William Whitelaw and for constructive comments on the early text drafts) and Stuart Sellar (who also kindly looked over early material and was, as always, most generous in helping in photograph research). Charles Gregory provided a unique insight into the operation of the LNER Cinema Car in 1935-36. Help is also acknowledged from Prof. Charles McKean, Stuart Rankin, Richard Lacey, Mike Macdonald, Hamish Stevenson and Brian D. Smith.

Particular thanks for help in finding illustrations go to Ronald Glendinning for making available pictures from the invaluable Montague Smith collection.

Errors and omissions are this author's responsibility entirely.

BOOKS *(Railway subjects)*

Allen, C.J. *ABC British express trains*. Nos.3 and 5. Ian Allan, 1960.

Bonavia, M.R. *A history of the LNER. I. The early years, 1923-33.* Allen & Unwin, 1982. ['*First years*' on cover].

Bonavia, M.R. *Railway policy between the wars.* Manchester University Press, 1981.

Carter, E.F. *Britain's railway liveries: colours, crests and linings, 1825-1948.* 2nd ed. Starke, 1963.

Cox, E.S. *Locomotive panorama.*Vols I and II. Ian Allan, 1965/66.

Crump, N. *By rail to victory.* LNER, 1947.

Dow, G. *The first railway across the Border.* LNER, 1946.

Ellis, C.H. *British railway history 1877-1947.* 1959.

Harris, M. *British main line services in the age of steam 1900-1968.* Haynes, 1996.

Hughes, G. *LNER.* Malaga Books (Ian Allan), 1986.

Hunter, D.L.G. *The Highland Railway in Retrospect.* Moorfoot, 1988.

International Union of Railways. *Main line railways of Great Britain, 1923-30.* 1931.

Johnston, C. and Hume, John R. *Glasgow Stations.* David & Charles, 1979.

Lamont, A. *How Scotland lost its railways.* SNP, 1945.

LMS. *A record of large-scale organisation and management, 1923-1946.* LMS, 1946.

McKillop, N. *Enginemen Elite.* Ian Allan, 1958.

Maclean, A.A. *North British Album.* Ian Allan, 1975.

Meacher, C. *LNER footplate memories.* Bradford Barton, [no date].

Mullay, A.J. *The Caledonian Railway 1844-1923.* Stenlake (in press).

Mullay, A.J. *The Castle and the Bear: a brief history of the NBR.* Stenlake (in press).

Nash, G.C. *The LMS at War.* LMS, 1946.

Nock, O.S. *The Highland Railway.* Ian Allan, 1965.

Nock, O.S. *A history of the LMS. 1. The first years, 1923-30.* Allen & Unwin, 1982.

Railway Correspondence and Travel Society. *Locomotives of the L.N.E.R.* (Various volumes).

Rolt, L.T.C. *Red for danger.* 4th edn. David & Charles, 1982.

Smith, D.L. *Legends of the Glasgow & South Western Railway in LMS days.* David & Charles, 1980.

Thomas, J. *The Callander & Oban Railway.* David & Charles, 1966.

Thomas, J. *The Springburn Story.* David & Charles, 2nd ed. 1974.

Vallance, H.A. *The Great North of Scotland Railway.* Vol.III. David St John Thomas, 1989.

BOOKS *(Non-railway transport subjects)*

Brodie, I. *Steamers of the Forth*. David & Charles, 1978.

Duckworth, C.L.D. and Langmuir, G.E. *Clyde river and other steamers*. 3rd edition. Brown, Son & Ferguson, 1972.

Grieves, R. *Scotland's motoring century*. XS Publications, 1999.

Hunter, D.L.G. *From SMT to Eastern Scottish: an 80th anniversary story*. Donald, 1987.

Stroud, J. *Railway Air Services*. Ian Allan, 1987.

Waugh, E. *Labels: a Mediterranean journal*. Penguin, 1985 [1930].

BOOKS *(Historical)*

Boyd, E. *Evacuation in Scotland; a record of events and experiments*. Scottish Council for Research in Education/University of London Press, 1944.

Garnett, M. and Aitken, I. *Splendid, splendid: the authorized biography of William Whitelaw*. [Grandson of LNER Chairman]. Cape, 2002.

Grieves, K. *Sir Eric Geddes: business and government in war and peace*. Manchester University Press, 1989.

Grigg, J. *Lloyd George, war leader, 1916-18*. Penguin, 2002.

Skelley, J. *The General Strike, 1926*. Lawrence & Wishart, 1976.

Symons, J. *The General Strike*. Ebury, 1987.

ARTICLES

LMS Railway Magazine (Various issues).

LNER Magazine (Various issues).

Meacher, C. 'The Gresley P2 Class'. *Gresley Observer*. 118, 1999, pp.61-62.

Mullay, A.J. 'How not to close a railway [Granton, 1925]'. *Railway World*, Vol.48, 870, 1987.

Mullay, A.J. and Coleford, I.C. 'The Tweed Valley Railway'. *Railway Bylines*. Summer Special 5, 2002, pp.4-25.

North Eastern & Scottish Magazine (LNER). 1923/24 volume.

Tatlow, P. 'The LMS in Scotland', *Backtrack* Vol.7 (1), 1993, pp.33-41.

Winkworth, D.W. 'Difficulties with "Bolero" engines'. *Backtrack*, Vol.9 (4), 1995, pp.180-182.

Wright, I.L. The Highland section of the LMS, 1939-1945'. *Backtrack*, Vol.9 (4), 1995, pp.201-208.

If you are interested in purchasing other books published by Tempus,
or in case you have difficulty finding any Tempus books in your local bookshop,
you can also place orders directly through our website

www.tempus-publishing.com